Go Abraham Go

Go Abraham Go

EARL P. McQUAY

ACCENT BOOKS
Denver, Colorado

MEMBER OF
EVANGELICAL CHRISTIAN
PUBLISHERS ASSOCIATION

ACCENT BOOKS
A division of B/P Publications
12100 W. Sixth Avenue
P.O. Box 15337
Denver, Colorado 80215

Copyright © 1977 B/P Publications, Inc.
Printed in U.S.A.

Library of Congress Number: 77-075130

ISBN 0-916406-68-7

Dedication

To
Rose,
my beloved

Two pilgrims,
called and led by Him,
together we journey
as one.

Contents

Contents

Introduction

Abraham was a man on the go! He left his familiar homeland to travel 1,000 miles to a strange country. He went out on "a march without a map, a progress without a program." Obeying the call of God, he broke the limits of today and traveled into the expanse of tomorrow. His journey of faith is described in the Biblical "Hall of Faith" epitaph: "By faith Abraham, when he was called to go out into a place which he should after receive for an inheritance, obeyed; and he went out, not knowing whither he went. . . . For he looked for a city which hath foundations, whose builder and maker is God" (Hebrews 11:8,10).

Man's basic aspirations and needs always have been the same, whether in 2000 B.C. or in A.D. 2000. The record of Abraham's dynamic life discoveries, now 4,000 years old, throbs with encouragement and challenge for the present-day Christian. In retracing the steps of Abraham, we uncover lessons that are vitally relevant for us today as they point us to the God of Abraham.

Chapter 1

Road Hazards

*T*here were many obvious reasons why a man born in the city of Ur should stay there. Ur, a major city of the Babylonian civilization, had some of the best homes in the world, multiple-roomed in contrast to the single-roomed abodes of Canaan. The Euphrates River skirted the city, and canals ran throughout its residential areas. Ur claimed some of the earliest libraries of the world. The first known medical prescription dates back to 2700 B.C. and was written by a man named Lulu of Ur. From the midst of Ur rose one of the famous ziggurats of Mesopotamia, a man-made mountain in the form of a terraced pyramid with each story smaller than the one below it. The entire city life revolved around the moon god, to whom the ziggurat was erected as a temple of worship.

The Babylonian civilization was at a peak of cultural and political splendor during Abraham's time. For several hundred years, Babylonia had enjoyed a high level of civilization with writing, highly developed arts, beautiful gems and carvings, and well-established law codes and legal systems. The people of Ur had developed a most attractive way of life for themselves. Anyone would have been tempted to stay there, even as a servant, and live on the leftovers of the lavish life.

Comfortably situated in Ur, Abraham one day heard a divine command to get up and go: "Get thee out of thy country . . . into the land which I shall shew thee" (Acts 7:3). Though a lot of sacrifice was involved, Abraham was obedient to the call of God.

Hearing the call of God, we may weigh many "disadvantages" of giving up what we have; but when God calls, He expects us to obey! Only by hearing and obeying the call of God was it possible for Abraham to become a great nation and a source of blessing to the world.

What motivated Abraham to break home ties and to move 1,000 miles to a strange land? He was moved by an astonishing promise from the eternal God—the "Abrahamic Covenant."

At various times in Biblical history, God issued a covenant to men. God's covenants with Noah, Abraham, Moses, and David in the Old Testament were sovereign administrations of grace and promise (Genesis 6:18-22; Genesis 12:1-3; Exodus 6:5-8; II Samuel 7:8-16). Each covenant was unconditional, was instituted of God, and was secured by the immutable character of God. There was a progressive enrichment in the covenants, each successive covenant presenting a fuller development of God's redemptive accomplishment that is present from the outset.

The grace exemplified in the older covenants is brought to its fullest exhibition and bestowal in the "New Covenant" provided by Jesus Christ (Matthew 26:28). Christ's New Covenant is the sum total of the grace, blessing, truth, and eternal relationship comprised in the redemption secured by His blood. It is designated as everlasting because it is not to be displaced by a more complete realization of what covenant grace embodies (Hebrews 12:28; 13:20).

Four beautiful dimensions of blessing were included in God's covenant with Abraham. First, God promised the possession of a *land*. "Get thee out of thy country . . . unto a land that I will show thee" (Genesis 12:1). Abraham would be given a great body of land that would belong to his descendants. That land lay in the center of the "Fertile Crescent," in the heart of the world, halfway between the Far East and the Far West. It was a fruitful land, into which God would triumphantly bring the nation of Israel about 700 years after Abraham was given the promise of the Hebrew nation as his descendants. Abraham dwelled in the new land for about a hundred years, yet he never owned more than a little burial plot he had bought from the Hittites, where he could lay Sarah's bones to rest. Abraham lived in Canaan, but he never owned the land. Yet his faith would be rewarded; all his descendants would be given the land.

The second dimension of God's covenant

was His promise to multiply Abraham's seed to become a *nation* of innumerable people. "I will make of thee a great nation" (verse 2). Already Abraham and Sarah were past the age of having children. But God promised to give him a great posterity.

Third, God promised *protection* to Abraham's posterity. "I will bless them that bless thee, and curse him that curseth thee" (verse 3a). For 4,000 years now, mankind has been a spectator of the divine preservation of the nation of Israel. The devil hates Israel, and has led nation after nation in persecuting her. In our century the persecution was epitomized in the holocaust of the 1940's — Adolph Hitler's endeavor to exterminate the Jews, and his successful destruction of an estimated six million of Abraham's seed. But God cut Hitler's arm short with His curse upon the enemy of His chosen nation.

Because of their disobedience to God when they lived in their own land, the Israelites have suffered ravage, dispersion, and persecution. In the end, however, Israel will be restored to her land and will recognize her Messiah, Jesus Christ, whom she rejected; and God will destroy her enemies, as he promised Abraham long ago. The Jewish people are a phenomenon to the world. They have a divine origin, a divine history, and a divinely predicted future.

The fourth aspect of God's covenant with Abraham is the capstone of divine prophecy. Out of one man, Abraham, would come *universal blessing.* "In thee shall all families of the earth be blessed" (verse 36). How can all the world be blessed through one man? The nation that came from him was to be a repository for the revelation of God. Through Abraham's descendants we have the Holy Scriptures! Also, the nation was to be a witness for God to the other nations of the earth. But greatest of all, through Israel was to come the "son of Abraham," Jesus Christ, God incarnate in human flesh, who was to provide salvation for all men who would be saved (Matthew 1:1). Abraham could have received no greater promise from God!

Joaquin Miller, in the tract "The Jew in Prophecy," reminds us of the blessings we owe to Abraham's descendants:

Who taught you tender Bible tales
Of honey lands, of milk and wine,
Of happy, peaceful Palestine,
Of Jordan's holy harvest vales?
Who gave the patient Christ, I say?
Who gave you Christian Creed? Yea, yea.
Who gave your very God to you?
Your Jew, your Jew, your hated Jew.

God has a world view; and when we respond to His call, He joins us to His world program. The promise of becoming a universal blessing is applicable to the follower of Jesus Christ today. Every Christian's life should fit into God's plan for the worldwide spread of the gospel. God's plan for us is not that missions should have a place in our lives, but that our lives may have a place in His world program of redemption. Where does your life fit into the work that God is performing in the world today?

We must be aware of hazards that line the road of obedience to God. The first threat Abraham faced was the hazard of *delay*.

God's call first came to Abraham in Ur of the Chaldees (Acts 7:2-4). In response, Abraham got out of Ur and went as far as Haran. This was a journey of 600 miles. But with his family Abraham settled down in Haran (Genesis 11:31). Life was good and easy in Haran; and Abraham seemed to forget that God had called him to Canaan, 400 miles farther than he had come. A second call to Abraham was needed to get him "out of the rut" (Genesis 12:1-3). The hazard of delay was overcome when Abraham "departed out of Haran" (verse 4).

The death of Abraham's father, Terah (Genesis 11:32), appears to be the occasion for Abraham's renewal of purpose. A crisis of sorrow broke the link with Haran and got Abraham on the move again. The loss of his father was a sad experience for Abraham; but the maxim was just as applicable then as it is now: "Disappointment is *His* appointment!" Through difficulties we face, we may see God's promises in a new way. There is an old Italian proverb: "When God shuts a door, He opens a window." Many a Christian pilgrim on the road of obedience has come to barriers which eventually have meant new and broader fields of service. God has a wonderful way of causing distressing circumstances to bring us into new discoveries of His rich plan for us.

Abraham could not let his life stop at Haran, where his father finished his course. Abraham was seeking something better. Stirred again by the voice of God, Abraham pressed onward toward the completion of his thousand-mile pilgrimage.

Abraham next faced the hazard of *difficulty*. The land of Canaan was not empty and

16

waiting for him to move in and take over. The land was divided among a varying number of Canaanite/Amorite city-states. The decadent Canaanite culture would not be able to co-exist with the emergent monotheistic culture of Abraham. These were the people who, generations later, would drive the descendants of Abraham, in unbelief and fear, back into the desert for nearly forty years of wandering.

Facing the difficulty of the Canaanites, Abraham might have considered the obstacles to be too threatening. But God, who is greater than the Canaanite, showed Himself to Abraham and gave him courage and inner strength. As soon as Abraham began taking note of the Canaanites (Genesis 12:6), God revealed Himself to Abraham again and repeated His great promise, "Unto thy seed will I give this land" (verse 7).

More than once when my wife and I have faced a great difficulty in our lives, we have cast our souls upon the Word of God; and in His promises we have found great refuge and strength to face our trials. "Greater is he that is in you, than he that is in the world," is God's assuring promise to us in I John 4:4. The promises of God outshine the problems of man.

Upon his arrival in Canaan, Abraham's first action was the building of an altar. In any dispensation, the top priority of the follower of God is to ". . . seek ye first the kingdom of God, and his righteousness" (Matthew 6:33). Near Bethel, Abraham "pitched his tent . . . and there he builded an altar unto the Lord, and called upon the name of the Lord" (Genesis 12:8). Abraham never built a house after he left Haran. In relation to the world,

Abraham was a pilgrim; he lived in a tent. In relation to God, he built an altar—these are the only things recorded that Abraham erected. Far better to have a tent and an altar in this world than to have a mansion without an altar.

Of all the land that God promised to Abraham—stretching from the Euphrates River in the north to the Negeb in the far south, and from the Jordan River to the Great Sea—do you know how much real estate Abraham actually owned in his lifetime? Only one little plot of ground, which he had purchased for a burial place. "These all died in faith, not having received the promises, but having seen them afar off, and were persuaded of them, and embraced them, and confessed that they were strangers and pilgrims on the earth" (Hebrews 11:13). As far as Abraham's earthly life was concerned, no city could claim him as its own. Wherever he pitched his tent, Abraham built an altar. He never found a permanent hometown in this world; but no matter where he was, he saw to it that the altar was built to God. You could have trailed him by going from altar to altar. Long after the tent was moved, the altar stood to show where the man of God had been.

A third hazard Abraham faced was the *diversion* that resulted when a famine arose in Canaan. Instead of "toughing it out" in the land where God had promised to care for him, Abraham made a poor decision. He turned to the wicked nation of Egypt, which throughout sacred history is a picture of the world and fleshly reliance. Did Abraham bow at his altar and pray for the Lord to provide his needs? No. He "went down into Egypt to sojourn there" (Genesis 12:10). Going to Egypt meant that Abraham fell into unbelief. It also meant that he would have to live in a basically false situation and would have to lie.

When Abraham went down into Egypt, he probably saw the Pyramid of Gizeh, which was already 700 years old. It still stands today as a monument to the vanity of man. Abraham had no desire to build a pyramid; but notice that he was unable to build an altar while he was in Egypt. Moving into Egypt in a state of unbelief, he was in no condition to worship God.

In Egypt, the weaker side of Abraham's character became manifest. For fear that some man of power in Egypt might kill him in order to take his beautiful wife, Sarah, Abraham resorted to carnal means of protecting himself rather than depending upon God to do so.

It was then common for men of power to confiscate beautiful women, and so the natural character of man—cowardice, deceit, distrust—now surfaced in Abraham's experience. He asked Sarah not to tell inquirers that she was his wife but to tell them that she was his sister (verses 11-13).

Actually, this was a half-truth for Sarah not only was Abraham's wife, she also was a half-sister to him (Genesis 20:12). But remember that a half-truth is a full lie! It may have the skin of a truth but it is stuffed with a lie. God has never promised to bless a lie. A lie is never justified in God's Word. Our Lord is Truth, and He wants us to be rid of deceit and to speak the truth always.

When Pharaoh favored Abraham in behalf of his "sister," God used plagues to bring the truth to light. When the Egyptian ruler discovered that Sarah was Abraham's wife instead of his sister, there was only one choice—namely, to send the whole clan away. Abraham and his family, therefore, were dispatched back to Canaan (Genesis 12:14-20).

The Bible is an honest book. It portrays the faults of its great men along with their strengths. In doing so it saves us from worshiping mere human beings, however great; and it also gives us hope for improvement in spite of our own failures. Even Abraham, the father of the faithful, was not always victorious. When we find ourselves struggling and failing in our Christian experience, we can find strength in the God of Abraham. Often, the Bible refers to the God of Abraham, and the emphasis is always not on Abraham but on the *God* of Abraham. Abraham's God was faithful in sparing him from self-destruction in his folly in Egypt. God brought Abraham back to Bethel.

Road Hazards

Go, Abraham, Go

Chapter 2

Decision at the Crossroads

*B*ack to Bethel came Abraham—back to the land of promise and back to the place of the altar. Abraham's weakness of faith was revealed in his trip to Egypt. But now his *renewal* of faith is seen in his return to Bethel (Genesis 13:1-4). Abraham returned to the scene of his former worship—probably for the purpose of expressing humility and penitence for his misconduct in Egypt, thankfulness for God's deliverance from perils, and renewal of allegiance to his covenant God.

Aren't there times in our lives when we find ourselves leaning upon Egypt and relying upon fleshly means to satisfy us—times when we must forsake Egypt and get back to our "Bethel," the place of spiritual renewal? Have you been diverted from the course of faith, and have you come back to the altar of commitment? It is at Bethel that the back-slider can exclaim, "He restoreth my soul: he leadeth me in the paths of righteousness for his name's sake" (Psalm 23:3).

"And Abram was very rich in cattle, in silver, and in gold" (Genesis 13:2). Because the Egyptian monarch did not take back the gifts he had bestowed as a dowry for Sarah, the gifts became the foundation of the immense wealth that Abraham was to accumulate. But "Lot also, which went with Abram, had flocks, and herds, and tents" (verse 5). The increase of wealth for Abraham and his nephew gave rise to further complications for Abraham.

A new problem arose for Abraham when his company settled again in the land of Canaan. There was discord among the servants of Abraham and Lot. Their herdsmen were wrangling constantly for the first use of the wells and the first crop of the pastures. Besides this, their cattle continually were getting mixed. "The land was not able to bear them, that they might dwell together: for their substance was great, so that they could not dwell together" (verse 6).

Abraham knew that the conflict must not be allowed to continue. He realized that the cause for the disturbance probably would lead to similar troubles continually. When the quarrels between the servants were reported to their masters, Abraham and Lot were susceptible to irritation with each other. For the sake of the testimony of God before the Canaanite and the Perizzite dwelling in the land, and because Abraham knew that internal conflict within his own tribe would make him vulnerable to destruction by the enemy, he made a wise proposal (verses 7-9).

Abraham's *reliance* of faith is seen in the

magnanimous decision that he made when he and Lot stood at the crossroads in Canaan. As the elder and the leader of the expedition, Abraham had the right to the first choice of land. But he waived his right in the interests of reconciliation.

"Lot, it's not right that our families should live in contention. Let's separate our men and choose different areas for our people. You choose your area, and then I'll settle in a different place. Each will have his own territory, and we will remain at peace with each other without having these wranglings among our servants."

To allow Lot to make the decision took grace for Abraham. Relinquishing his patriarchal privilege, Abraham submitted himself to the will of God in a great act of faith. In the time of famine, he had made his own decision, and near tragedy resulted. Now with reliance of faith, he determined to let Lot make the first decision, and to let God decide which path he should follow. Rather than choose for himself, Abraham trusted God to choose for him. One who is sure of God can afford to hold very lightly the things of this world.

> *Not mine—not mine the choice*
> *In things of great or small;*
> *Be thou my Guide, my Guard, my*
> *Strength,*
> *My wisdom and my "All."*

Because Abraham's nephew, Lot, was more a follower of Abraham than a follower of God, he became a burden to Abraham. Lot was an alloy that clung to the metal, and now the process of separation became necessary. To this point we are told repeatedly that Lot went with Abraham, but this record would not be made again (Genesis 12:5; 13:1,5). Lot could not stand the stress of a life of separation to God; he became, therefore, a hindrance to Abraham. In our activity with God, we must examine ourselves and prove that we move because of love for Him and are not "going along for the ride."

When Abraham forced Lot's hand, their relationship was severed. Not all ties were broken but they did go their separate ways. We sometimes have to face the fact that if a person does not make a change, we therefore have to break our yoke with him. Hosea declared of the tribe of Ephraim: He "is joined to idols: let him alone" (Hosea 4:17). In relation to persons living according to the flesh, Paul admonished the Corinthian Christians to "come out from among them and be ye separate" (II Corinthians 6:17). When a person has determined to follow the will of God, it is inevitable that some links in his life will need to be snapped—perhaps a companionship must be forsaken, or perhaps a habit must be dropped.

Lot had been a camp-follower, going along with his uncle because of material benefits. But Lot could not resist the temptation to exploit his uncle. When the situation got out of control, Abraham had to draw the line. Sometimes a human relationship has to be severed for the sake of something better in the will of God. It is better to lose than to win if in winning you pitch your tent toward Sodom.

Every person faces in his life the crossroads

that Abraham and Lot faced. In Canada there stands over a little stream of water a marker that identifies the spot as "The Great Divide." There one part of the stream moves toward the west, joining other streams and rivers to end up in the Pacific Ocean. The other part of the original stream winds its way in a different direction, eventually joins the Mississippi River, and culminates its journey in the Gulf of Mexico. At the point of "the great divide" in our lives we make a decision, and that decision determines our destiny. Standing at the great divide, every one answers for himself the question, "Will I go my way or will I go God's way?"

Lot's decision revealed an attitude that had long been his problem. His land choice was simply the occasion for the manifestation of a worldly bent of soul. From the beginning, evidently, the polarity of Lot's soul was self-ward instead of God-ward. Given the opportunity to make the decision of land choice, he went the way of the flesh and pitched his tent in the direction of Sodom, one of the most wicked cities of the world in that day.

In an honest appraisal of your heart attitude, do you find yourself to be like Lot? Perhaps you've followed along with someone else who follows God—your parents, your wife or husband, or some friend. It seemed to be the right thing to do and so you did it. But deep down in your heart you have to admit that your soul, like Lot's, has been bent toward the green fields of Sodom rather than toward the will of God. As Paul admonishes us, "Examine yourselves, whether ye be in the faith; prove your own selves" (II Corinthians 13:5).

Many have followed the path of Lot in the direction of Sodom because their souls were attracted to the things of this world rather than to the things of God. Paul's sad comment on one young man was, "Demas hath forsaken me, having loved this present world, and is departed unto Thessalonica" (II Timothy 4:10).

As a speaker declared at the LeTourneau College baccalaureate service some time ago, "Many start, but few finish." How have you fared in your journey with God since that day you first set out to follow His will? Abraham and Lot started well; but Lot didn't end well. His worldly inclination got him into a miserable situation.

Lot's choice was made out of selfish ambition. Turning his face in the direction of evil's attraction, Lot became "a bad lot." Benjamin Franklin once declared, "There are two passions which have a powerful influence in the affairs of men. These are ambition and avarice: the love of power and the love of money. Separately, each of these has great force in prompting man to action; but when united in view of the same object they have in many minds the most violent effects."

Notice how swiftly Lot was drawn into the whirlpool. To begin with, he looked in the direction of Sodom (Genesis 13:10). Then he chose the plain, journeyed eastward, and separated himself from Abraham (verse 11). Next, he "dwelled in the cities of the plain, and pitched his tent toward Sodom" (verse 12). Finally, we read that he "sat in the gate of Sodom," indicating that he had become a member of the municipal council (Genesis 19:1). We can clearly see the downward path of a man whom God later would have to "burn out" of his self-imposed predicament.

When "Lot chose him all the plain of Jordan," he did not inquire of God concerning His will (Genesis 13:11). He did not consider the possible effect that the moral condition of Sodom would have upon his children or his own life. Lot's decision was a self-centered one determined by lust.

Sodom was a wicked city, filled with base, unnatural fleshly practices. "But the men of Sodom were wicked and sinners before the Lord exceedingly" (verse 13). The New Testament tells us that Sodom is "set forth for an example, suffering the vengeance of eternal fire" (Jude 7) and is "an ensample unto those that after should live ungodly" (II Peter 2:6).

If God sends a man to Sodom, He will protect him there, as He protected Daniel when He sent him to Babylon. But if God does not send a man to Sodom, the man makes a serious blunder if he goes there. Unable to see past the pretty fields, Lot cut himself out of Canaan, and eventually brought destruction upon his household in Sodom.

What a contrast we see between Lot and Abraham as they stood at the crossroads. Lot was moved by selfishness, Abraham by unselfishness. Lot said, "I'll choose." Abraham said, "I'll let God choose for me." Lot had this world at heart and walked by sight; Abraham had the heavenly world at heart and walked by faith. Lot chose the "best" and ended in the City of Condemnation; Abraham took what was left and settled in the Land of Promise.

The decision was made! Now what? Alone

and reflecting upon the crossroads now passed, Abraham may have had occasion to question the decision that he had made. When Abraham was left with the lonely feeling that naturally resulted from Lot's departure, God chose that desolate day as the opportune time to reveal His reward for Abraham's faith. One cannot always understand why God allows reversals to come his way. But one thing is sure—hardships are part of the heavenly Father's plan for our spiritual development.

A Christian young man invested all his savings in a peach orchard in a year when the trees gave promise of a bountiful crop. Then came a killing frost that ruined his entire crop. Embittered, he quit attending church. Visited by his pastor, he said, "I'm not coming anymore because I cannot worship a God who cares for me so little that He would let the frost destroy my peaches!" The wise pastor replied, "The Lord loves *you* more than your crop. He knows that while fruit does better without chilling winds, it is impossible to produce Christian character without the frosts of trial! God's primary concern is to develop strong men, not lovely peaches!" Our trials may seem severe, but God kindly uses them to fit us for His blessing and service. He allows trials, not to impair us, but to improve us.

Abraham's faith allowed God to fix the inheritance in his life. He had blundered in going to Egypt; he would not now make a similar mistake. On the hill near Bethel, looking across the plains of the Dead Sea, Abraham entrusted his future to God.

Abraham experienced a lesson that was illustrated in modern times at the Dead Sea.

While walking along its shores one day, a man lost his balance and fell into the water at a point where it was deep. Not being a swimmer, he was panic-stricken, and thrashed about with his arms and legs, fearing he would sink and drown. At last completely exhausted, he felt he could do no more and he ceased from his strivings. Crying out to God for help, he prepared for the worst. To his great surprise, as soon as he relaxed, the water bore him up. The Dead Sea is so full of salt and other minerals that a person can easily float upon its surface. He will not drown when he resigns himself to the buoyancy of the water.

Abraham found the everlasting arms of God upheld him when he relinquished his unnecessary fears and ceased from his own carnal efforts. The safety and serenity offered by such a complete reliance on God quieted his heart in an hour of difficulty.

I have often been comforted while thinking of these words:

He knows, He loves, He cares;
Nothing this truth can dim.
God gives His best to those
Who leave the choice with Him.

"And the Lord said unto Abraham, after that Lot was separated from him, Lift up now thine eyes, and look from the place where thou art northward, and southward, and eastward, and westward: For all the land which thou seest, to thee will I give it, and to thy seed for ever" (Genesis 13:14,15).

In a time when Abraham most needed a word from God, the Lord spoke to him and repeated His promise of a great land, a great nation, and a great future. God rewarded Abraham's faith and sealed His promise to Abraham again. In surrendering Sodom, Abraham had received something more wonderful. God never calls us to give up what is good for us: "For the Lord God is a sun and shield: the Lord will give grace and glory: no good thing will he withhold from them that walk uprightly" (Psalm 84:11).

A gentleman once addressed one of the "ragged schools" of London on the subject of faith. One young boy couldn't understand and asked for a further explanation of the meaning of faith. "Would you meet me tomorrow morning at 10 o'clock at King's Cross?" the speaker requested of the boy. The boy agreed, and met him punctually the next day.

"What do you want? How did you know I'd be here?" the man inquired of the boy.

The boy replied, "You said you'd tell me the meaning of faith. You asked me to meet you here at this time; and I didn't think that you would deceive me."

The man replied, "Well, my boy, that's faith!"

God had promised to bless Abraham, and Abraham dared to take God at His word. When he let God lead, he witnessed God's blessing. Meeting God anew at Bethel, Abraham again "built there an altar unto the Lord" (Genesis 13:18).

The type of submission that Abraham learned is clearly expressed in these words of J. A. W. Hamilton:

I do not ask the furnace fire to shun,
I would not flee;

Decision at the Crossroads

I only ask that Thou Thyself wilt come
  And walk with me.

I do not ask that all my way to Heaven
  Be hours of ease;
I only beg that every task I'm given
  Christ oversees.

I only ask that all my life may be
  With Thee bound up;
And what Thy loving hand doth mix for me
  Be in my cup.

Then all that's dark will be illum'ed
  with love.
  And all that's bright
Be but a foretaste of my joy above
  When faith wins sight.

Chapter 3

Progress in the Journey

*G*od promised to make Abraham great, and now Abraham began to experience some of the victories of that greatness. While Lot suffered defeat in Sodom, Abraham was enjoying the blessing of the Lord in Mamre.

Abraham's greatness is realized first in his *victory in battle*. For the first time we see Abraham in the unexpected character of a warrior. He assumes the role of a fighter to rescue his nephew Lot, who was captured during an attack upon his adopted city of Sodom.

The king of Elam, Chedorlaomer, had control for thirteen years over a number of cities that bordered on the Dead Sea. Five of these cities, including Sodom and Gomorrah, rebelled against Chedorlaomer (Genesis 14:1-4).

Chedorlaomer rounded up the armies of his

and three other cities, and invaded the territories of the unmanageable cities. This is the first war mentioned in the Bible. The Napoleon of his day, Chedorlaomer swept down through the valley, plundered the cities, and carried away everyone who was unfortunate enough to get in the way. Leave it to Lot to be in the wrong place at the right time—he was captured. Chedorlaomer defeated the men of Sodom and the other cities, finding the nature of the ground favoring his armies. Victorious, he took home with him a large amount of booty and a number of captives, including Lot (verses 5-12).

News of Lot's plight reached Abraham through an escapee. "When Abram heard that his brother was taken captive" (verse 14), he might have excused himself from taking any active concern in his nephew now that they were separated. But Abraham, far from rendering evil for evil, resolved to take immediate measures for Lot's rescue.

C. H. Mackintosh has explained what motivated Abraham to act: "Genuine faith, while it always renders us independent, never renders us indifferent; it will never wrap itself up in its fleece while a brother shivers in the cold" (from *Notes on the Book of Genesis*).

We must be willing to get involved when a brother is in need, as Paul admonished: "Brethren, if a man be overtaken in a fault, ye which are spiritual, restore such an one in the spirit of meekness; considering thyself, lest thou also be tempted. Bear ye one another's burdens, and so fulfill the law of Christ" (Galatians 6:1,2).

Three kinds of faith in Christ have been described by Dwight L. Moody: *struggling faith*, which is like a man in deep water; *clinging faith*, which is like a man hanging to the side of a boat; and *resting faith*, which finds a man safely within the boat, and able to reach out with a hand to help someone else.

Abraham left his own impregnable position and went out to save his nephew, who now had no rightful claim on him. Our victories are won, not when we stay within our own selves or family, or community or church— but when we leave the security that surrounds us and go out to help someone else. By doing so, we sometimes get badly hurt, but that is also when we win our biggest battles.

That Abraham now had a large establishment is seen in the fact that he could spare 318 slaves for battle while leaving a sufficient number to take care of the flocks (Genesis 14:14).

Waiting till Chedorlaomer's armies were asleep at night, Abraham's army rushed upon the enemy from different directions and defeated them in the panic that ensued (verses 15,16). Pursuing the frayed mob as far as Hobah in the north, Abraham rescued the goods and the people who had been seized, and brought them, with Lot, back to their cities. Abraham was victor! His great God was proving His all-sufficiency as Abraham moved on in His will.

A young man who had served in a job dusting Shinto idols in his earlier years testified to missionary Roger Hosier that his determination always had been that when he grew up he would find the god who "could dust his own self off." Only the God of Abraham is that God. He can take care of Himself and us!

Yesterday He helped me;
  Today He is the same.
How long will this go on?
  Forever, Praise His Name!

Abraham's greatness is next seen in his *blessing from Melchizedek*. "Just who was Melchizedek?" was the question I was asked out of the blue in a discussion period during an adult retreat. That's an interesting question! Named only once in this passage, Melchizedek is referred to later in both Testaments as a person of great significance.

Melchizedek was the king of Salem (Jerusalem) and priest of God who greeted Abraham on his return from the rout of Chedorlaomer (verses 18-20). Evidently, Melchizedek was the only one of the kings of Canaan who worshiped "the most high God, possessor of heaven and earth" (verse 19). To Melchizedek Abraham presented a tithe of the booty that he had taken from the enemy. In the giving of tithes to God's priest, Abraham acknowledged God's grace in giving him the victory.

One thousand years after Abraham, David, by his conquest of Jerusalem, became heir to Melchizedek's dynasty of priest-kings. David was acclaimed by divine oath as "a priest for ever after the order of Melchizedek" (Psalm 110:4).

In another one thousand years, Christ, the Son of David, was declared to be "a priest for ever after the order of Melchisedec" (Hebrews 7:17,21). The superiority of Christ and His new order to the Levitical order was thus established.

Although appearing and disappearing suddenly, with no record of his birth or descent given, Melchizedek fulfilled a role superior to that of Abraham and, by implication, to the Aaronic priesthood ascended from Abraham. He serves as an important picture of Jesus Christ, the eternal Priest and King. We need not suppose that Melchizedek was literally without father, mother, beginning of days, or end of life (verse 3). The point is that information on these points is shrouded in obscurity in order that the Scriptures might provide a clearer approximation of the character of Jesus Christ, the Ancient of Days. Although Christ was made after the order of Melchizedek, we best understand the type when we see that Melchizedek was "made like unto the Son of God" (verse 3).

Notice the ways in which the type, Melchizedek, compares with the archetype, Jesus Christ: 1) Melchizedek had no record of beginning or ending; Christ is the eternal Son of God. 2) Melchizedek was a priest before the Aaronic priesthood began; Christ is our Great High Priest from before the world began. 3) Melchizedek was the King of Salem (which means "peace"); Christ is the Prince of Peace who will return to reign at Jerusalem. 4) The name "Melchizedek" means "king of righteousness"; Christ is our righteousness and justification. 5) Melchizedek brought to Abraham bread and wine; Christ gave to us these elements in the Lord's Supper. 6) Melchizedek blessed Abraham in the Name of "the most high God"; in Christ we are blessed "with all spiritual blessings in heavenly places" (Ephesians 1:3). 7) Abraham paid tithes to Melchizedek; to Christ we present our whole lives as His stewards. 8) Melchizedek met Abraham following the battle; at the Second Coming of Christ, the Church Militant will become the Church Triumphant.

Amid the storm and wreckage of his times, Melchizedek reigned in his peaceful city, with war raging without. We live in a world ravaged by war, sin, and suffering. But we have peace in Christ. We have a word from our righteous King, who Himself one day will reign in Jerusalem. The word that we hear above the moans of creation is: "Let not your heart be troubled: ye believe in God, believe also in me. . . . I will come again, and receive you unto myself; that where I am, there ye may be also" (John 14:1,3).

Abraham won an even greater victory after the war! A third indication of his greatness is seen in his *refusal of Sodom's reward.* When the king of Sodom met Abraham and had the audacity to offer him the reward of all the goods he had rescued, Abraham refused (Genesis 14:17,21).

Though he had accepted the blessing from the king of Salem, he could not accept the proposition of the king of Sodom. Melchizedek's blessing effectually prepared Abraham to meet the king of Sodom. In refusing the offer, Abraham indicated that the blessing of Melchizedek was all that his heart desired. In his reply, he named God in the same words Melchizedek had used: "I have lift up mine hand unto the Lord, the most high God, the possessor of heaven and earth" (verse 22).

Quick to perceive the danger of receiving gifts from the king of Sodom, Abraham declared, "I will not take . . . any thing that is thine, lest thou shouldest say, I have made Abram rich" (verse 23). Not denying others the rights he denied himself, Abraham

40

allowed a portion of the spoils to go to the young men who had served with him in the battle (verse 24). But he would take nothing for himself. By his answer he showed that his soul was not for sale.

Abraham refused to be governed by the power of the world from which he sought to deliver Lot. He had trusted Egypt once to his detriment; now he would not depend on Sodom. His dependence was upon God!

The world will readily offer us its subsidies so as to bring us under obligation to its control. May we always beware of the ensnaring forms Satan uses to alienate our affection for our Lord. We must not look for our reward in Sodom; our blessing comes from our "most high God, the possessor of heaven and earth."

Why Thou couldst ever love me so,
And be the God Thou art,
Is darkness to my intellect,
But sunshine to my heart.

Chapter 4

The Direction Is Set

*T*he excitement of the military campaign was over and Abraham was back in Mamre. He might easily have become a prey to despondency and terror at the thought that the nations he had defeated would muster new forces against him. As he anticipated future needs, he might also have had second thoughts about his rejection of the goods offered to him by the king of Sodom. To dispel his fears, God made a gracious announcement to him.

"Fear not, Abram: I am thy shield, and thy exceeding great reward" were the opening words of God's promise (Genesis 15:1). Those comforting words, "Fear not," appearing here for the first time, occur 180 times in the Scriptures. Often the child of God in assailable situations needs to hear these words from

God. God is both our "shield" (protector from ill in the negative aspects of life) and our "reward" (provider of all good things in the positive aspects of life).

For Abraham, the direction was set. He was going with God. And God spoke to him. God's promise to Abraham included an heir and an estate. An heir without an estate would have been only half a promise; and an estate without an heir would have been meaningless. But God provided both.

God's *promise of an heir* answered Abraham's question that emanated from a spirit of fretfulness, "Lord God, what wilt thou give me, seeing I go childless, and the steward of my house is this Eliezer of Damascus?" (verses 2,3). Abraham wondered how God's promise of a seed would be fulfilled. Abraham had no son, and apparently his adopted heir was his slave, Eliezer.

Excavations at Nuzi in Iraq provide useful background information regarding the patriarchal age. One large group of documents uncovered at Nuzi deals with inheritance. The estate normally passed to the eldest son, who received a "double portion" of that given to the younger. Should a man have no son, he could adopt one. The adopted son was expected to care for the man in his old age, to provide proper burial, and to continue the family name in exchange for the property.

God immediately answered Abraham and assured him that he would have a son of his own who would fulfill the promise (verses 4,5). Furthermore, out of Abraham would come a great nation of people, as great in number as the stars of the heavens.

"And he believed in the Lord; and he

counted it to him for righteousness" (verse 6). Here is the formula for man's appropriation of God's salvation—faith. This verse is quoted twice in the New Testament as a proof-text for justification through faith without human works (Romans 4:1-5; Galatians 3:6-9), and once to show that saving faith results in works (James 2:20-24).

The statement of Abraham's faith was chosen by the Holy Spirit as the model of justification by faith. Abraham believed that God would fulfill His promise in giving him a son. He was saved by faith. Before the coming of Christ, a person was saved by believing the promise of God; since Calvary, a person is saved by believing that God's promise of salvation was fulfilled at the cross.

"And the scripture, foreseeing that God would justify the heathen through faith, preached before the gospel unto Abraham, saying, In thee shall nations be blessed" (Galatians 3:8). The "gospel" is not strictly New Testament teaching. The gospel was presented in seed form in the garden of Eden (Genesis 3:15). The gospel was given also to Abraham when God promised him that through his seed all the nations of the earth would be blessed. Abraham didn't realize the full implications of that promise, but he trusted in God and believed His Word to the extent that he could comprehend it; and his faith was accounted as righteousness. To say that men in Old Testament days were saved by keeping the law, in contrast to salvation by faith in New Testament days, is erroneous. Man in any age was and is justified by faith alone.

Missionary David Morse often had witnessed to Rambhau, an Indian pearl diver

with whom he had established a close friendship. "Free salvation for anyone who simply
believes in Christ is where your good religion
breaks down," Rambhau would respond.
"Sahib Morse, I cannot accept that. Perhaps I
am too proud. I must work for my place in
Heaven, or I would always be uncomfort-
able."

When Rambhau's retirement came, he prepared to make a 900-mile religious pilgrimage
to Delhi on his knees. He could not be
dissuaded by Morse, and insisted that the
suffering and blood poisoning or leprosy that
possibly could result from the trip would be
sweet and would purchase Heaven for him.

Before he was to leave for Delhi, Rambhau
presented to Morse a large pearl with the
explanation, "My son was a diver, too. He had
the swiftest dive, the keenest eye, and the
longest breath of any man who sought for
pearls. What joy he brought to me! He always
dreamed of finding a pearl beyond all that
had ever been found. One day he found it.
But when he saw it, he had already been
under water too long. He lost his life soon
after. All these years I have kept the pearl;
but now I am going, not to return, and to
you, my best friend, I am giving my pearl."

For a moment the missionary was speech-
less and gazed with awe at the mammoth,
brilliant pearl. A new thought came to him,
and he looked up quickly.

"Rambhau," he said, "this is a wonderful
pearl. Let me buy it. I would give you ten
thousand dollars for it."

"Sahib," replied Rambhau, "no man in the
world has money enough to pay what this
pearl is worth to me. I will not sell it to you.

You may only have it as a gift."

"No, Rambhau, as much as I want the pearl, I cannot accept it that way. Perhaps I am proud, but that is too easy. I must pay for it."

The old pearl diver was stunned. "You don't understand, sahib. Don't you see? My only son gave his life to get this pearl, and I wouldn't sell it for any money. You can only accept it as a gift."

The missionary was choked and for a moment could not speak. Then he gripped the hand of the old man.

"Rambhau," he urged in a low voice, "don't you see? That is just what you have been saying to God."

The diver looked long and searchingly at the missionary and slowly he began to understand as the missionary explained: "God is offering to you salvation as a free gift. It is so great and priceless that no man on earth could do anything to deserve it. Rambhau, of course I will accept the pearl in deep humility, praying God I may be worthy of your love. Rambhau, won't you accept God's great gift of Heaven, too, in deep humility, knowing it cost Him the death of His Son to offer it to you?"

Tears were coursing down the old man's cheeks. The great veil was lifting. He understood at last, and accepted God's free gift of eternal life through faith.

God promised a son to Abraham, and Abraham said, "Lord, I believe you." God's word to us today is, "I have given you My Son. He died for you on the cross of Calvary. Believe in Him and you will be saved." Abraham believed God. You and I also must believe God to be counted righteous in His sight.

God's *promise of an estate* followed His promise of a son for Abraham (Genesis 15:7-21). Not only would God make of Abraham a great people, but to that people He would give a great land. The land would include all the land of Canaan stretching "from the river of Egypt unto the great river, the river Euphrates" (verses 18-21).

"Lord God, whereby shall I know that I shall inherit it?" (verse 8). Delighted by the explicit promise of Canaan, Abraham requested a sign from God. God confirmed His promise by a remarkable ceremony.

God commanded Abraham to prepare a sacrifice. Abraham slew the animals specified by God for the sacrifice, and divided them so that he could enter into covenant relationship with God (verses 9,10).

On occasions of great importance, Chaldean parties who joined in a compact would walk through the halves of a slain animal. And they would invoke a lamp as their witness. But in this case, only God passed between the halves. God caused Abraham to fall into a deep sleep before He walked between the sacrifices. Thus the covenant was one-sided—it applied to God alone. The covenant was totally dependent upon the integrity of God and not upon Abraham and his seed. Though Israel many times has failed God, God has never gone back on His promise to Abraham, because His was an unconditional covenant.

When the sacrifice was prepared, the birds of the air tried to steal the meat but Abraham drove them off (verse 11). The birds picture Satan, who would attempt to snatch away the promises of God and cause us to doubt Him.

We must drive off all doubts as to the faithfulness of God to fulfill His promises.

God told Abraham that his seed would end up in Egypt, "a land that is not theirs, and shall serve them; and they shall afflict them four hundred years" (verse 13). This is a prophecy of the Egyptian bondage, out of which Moses was to deliver Israel. "And afterward shall they come out with great substance" (verse 14).

"And it came to pass, that, when the sun went down, and it was dark, behold a smoking furnace, and a burning lamp that passed between those pieces" (verse 17). Many of our deepest spiritual experiences come when darkness invades our lives. God showed Abraham that all would not be bright in the future of his posterity. A smoking furnace and a burning lamp; a furnace of affliction and a lamp of testimony—this was to be Israel's continuous experience.

Israel spent 400 years in the smoking furnace of bondage in Egypt; and then God brought His people forth as a shining light. In the Period of the Judges, and again in the Assyrian and Babylonian captivities, God allowed His chosen people to pass through the furnace. But each time they came out as a shining light. In the Church Age, Israel has been in the furnace. But at the Second Coming of Christ, Israel will be revived spiritually and will shine again!

The furnace and the lamp both are representative of experiences common to all God's children. It is true that "God had one Son without sin; but never one without suffering." God purifies us in the furnace of trial in order that our lamps may shine more brightly for

Him. The greatest pain that my wife and I have borne in our experiences has effected the greatest growth in our spiritual lives. Charles Spurgeon said of the furnace experience, "As sure as God ever puts His children into the furnace, He will be in the furnace with them."

A farmer in Maine was building a sturdy stone wall before the coming of the blustery New England winter. A tourist observing the construction asked about its strange dimensions, a height of four feet and a width of five feet. With "tongue in cheek" the industrious fence-maker replied, "I built it like this so that if it ever blows over, it will be taller than it was before." A good lesson can be drawn from the farmer's humorous comment. God is looking for saints who, when they are blown over by tribulation, become taller than they were before.

When trials come and you feel choked and blinded by the smoking furnace, don't let it turn you from God, but let it drive you closer to God. Remember the declaration of Job: "But he knoweth the way that I take: when he hath tried me, I shall come forth as gold" (Job 23:10). The advantage of the furnace experience has been affirmed by George Mueller, who said, "The only way to learn strong faith is to endure strong trials."

In Bradenton, Florida, my family visited the plant of Tropicana Industries, the largest producer of fresh citrus juice in America. It is amazing what Tropicana does with the thousands of oranges that are rolled onto its conveyor belts daily. One machine squeezes the juice; another machine makes additional extractions for the essence of women's perfume; and another machine produces cattle feed from the remaining rind and pulp. Once a visitor commented to Tropicana President Anthony Rossi, "Mr. Rossi, when an orange sees you, it must turn pale with fear." Mr. Rossi's quick reply was, "No, the orange smiles because it knows that it is going to get the greatest use possible!"

When we face trial and difficulty, our natural inclination is to turn pale with fear. But when we understand God's ways, we learn to view trials differently. Pain is not our enemy; it is our teacher. In the midst of its smoke, our souls develop.

Chapter 5

Detour of Unbelief

*H*ad it been anyone else besides Sarah who made the suggestion, Abraham likely would have been more vigilant. But he found it difficult to discern the wrong of the temptation when it came from his own dear wife. And her suggestion appealed so well to his distrusting fear. The man of faith took a detour of unbelief when he submitted to the persuasion of Sarah to have a child through her servant, Hagar.

Three characteristics of unbelief are seen in Abraham's act with Hagar. First, it is obvious that *unbelief is impatient.* God calls upon faith to be still and to wait upon Him to accomplish His purpose in His way. But Satan tempts us toward unbelief, which cries out: "I can't wait for God, I must do things my way; I must act quickly or it will be too late!"

Abraham was now eighty-five years old and already had spent ten years in Canaan (Genesis 16:3,16). God had promised Abraham a child, and through the child a nation, and through the nation a blessing for the whole world. But time was passing, and Abraham and Sarah were getting old.

Abraham's faith now was tested in the sixth way, according to A. W. Pink in his *Gleanings in Genesis* (pp. 174,175). The fervor of his faith had been tested when he was called to leave his home and kindred. The sufficiency of his faith had been tested when he was required to look to God to supply during the famine. The humility of his faith had been tested when he was led to yield to Lot's decision in the choice of land. The boldness of his faith had been seen in his campaign to rescue Lot from Chedorlaomer. The dignity of his faith had been revealed in his refusal to accept honors from the king of Sodom. And now the patience of his faith was tested when he was required to wait for God to fulfill His promise of a son.

Faith must be patient and must accept God's delay. He knows the path that is best in our lives. But unbelief hates to wait. Unbelief is discontent with God's manner of fulfilling His promise. Our prayers are often like that of one young man: "Lord, give me patience, and give it to me right now!"

When James A. Garfield was president of Hiram College, he received the complaint of a father who looked over the four-year course: "Mr. Garfield, I don't believe my son will have time to take all that. Could you provide him with a shorter course?" The genial Garfield replied, "Why, yes, I think I can. You see, it all depends on what you want to make of him. When God wants an oak, He takes hundreds of years; but when He wants a squash, it requires only three months."

Unbelief demands that we act quickly and do things our way. Faith grows when we lose confidence in our clever abilities. Faith demands that we wait patiently and trust God to accomplish His purpose in His way. Even when it appears that God is silent in our lives we must trust Him to fulfill His good promise.

Following World War II the following words were found written on the wall of a cellar in Cologne, Germany:

I believe in the sun, even when it
is not shining;
I believe in love, even when I feel
it not;
I believe in God, even when He is
silent.

Have you experienced a time in your life when it appeared that God was silent? Faith must speak out in such an experience and declare, "I believe in God, even when He is silent." For God is still alive and working, even in the silence. He is accomplishing His purpose in His way, and when our faith is tried it must be patient. Silence is a part of His loving plan also.

Second, *unbelief resorts to human means.* Abraham's failure consisted of his attempt to further the purposes of God by human contrivance. When there appeared on the human level no likelihood that God's promise would be fulfilled, Sarah suggested to Abraham: "Behold now, the Lord hath restrained me from bearing: I pray thee, go in unto my maid; it may be that I may obtain children by her" (Genesis 16:2).

Marriage contracts dug up in Nuzi indicate that in the wedding vow a woman promised to give her husband children. Sometimes the contract stated that if she couldn't produce a child she would provide one through her handmaid. The contract was signed by the bride and by witnesses. Such an arrangement provided a means for the wife to recover from the embarrassment and disgrace customarily felt by a wife who could not have a son for her husband. Yet this procedure never has been a part of God's plan for marriage. But at this point in our consideration of Abraham's life, more important than the immorality of his action is the unbelief that was involved.

One would wonder how Abraham could vacillate so between faith and unbelief—until one looks within his own heart and life and realizes how typical this is of himself. We are encouraged to take heart when we realize that even such a great man as Abraham sometimes failed God in unbelief. In view of this, Paul declares, "Wherefore let him that thinketh he standeth take heed lest he fall" (I Corinthians 10:12). And should we fall, we must not give up; we must *get up!* How descriptive of the heart need of all of us is the prayer of the demoniac boy's father: "Lord, I believe; help thou mine unbelief" (Mark 9:24).

Abraham acted in unbelief when he consented to Sarah's scheme to have a child through Hagar (Genesis 16:4). It was a wrong step, indicating a lack of simple reliance on God; and Sarah was the first to reap the bitter fruit of her plan.

Third, *unbelief causes trouble.* Abraham and Sarah sought to accomplish God's purpose through fleshly means, and that never works out right. Seeking to do God's work in man's way spells trouble. Instead of bringing a blessing, Abraham's action wrought in unbelief became a source of grief. What a bitter thing it is to remove ourselves from the place of absolute dependence upon God. The consequences of unbelief are calamitous.

Abraham began to reap the harvest of his folly almost immediately in the division of his own household. Bitterness sprang up between Sarah and Hagar, and ultimately Hagar fled from Sarah's presence (Genesis 16:5-8).

God met Hagar with tenderness in the wilderness when she fled from Sarah, and promised her that she would have a son, "Ishmael," who would father a prolific line (verses 9-12). The description of Ishmael as a wild, unruly, warlike man is predictive of the turbulent and plundering character of the Arabs, Ishmael's descendants.

The birth of Ishmael, Hagar's son, memorialized Abraham's doubt! The far-reaching result of Abraham's action is found in the story of Ishmael's posterity—a constant source of trouble to Isaac's descendants. The modern Arab bloc stretches from the Atlantic Ocean to the Persian Gulf and includes Arabic-speaking peoples of nineteen countries. And the conflict between the Arabs and the Jews today is a source of international tension.

Ishmael grew up in Mecca where, centuries later, Mohammed was born. This descendant of Ishmael became the founder of the Islamic religion, a great enemy to both Judaism and

Christianity. Today there are nearly 500 million Muslims in the world. They worship a god, but not the true God revealed in Jesus Christ.

Think of the burden brought into the world because of Abraham's one act of unbelief. We can't realize the proportions of the danger we bring into our lives when for a moment we turn away from God and act in man's way rather than in God's way.

When Ishmael was about sixteen, a great celebration was held at the weaning of the child Isaac. Ishmael gave vent to his jealousy by mocking Isaac (Genesis 21:8,9). The Apostle Paul builds upon this act an extended allegory of the opposition of legalistic religionists to those who are born of the Spirit (Galatians 4:21-31).

Sarah was a freewoman; Hagar a slave. Isaac was the child of promise; Ishmael a child of fleshly endeavor. Through Isaac came the Saviour; but through Ishmael came persecution for Isaac's seed; therefore, Ishmael was cast out.

The Law proceeded from Sinai and Jerusalem, and like Hagar is a source of bondage; but Christ came from the Jerusalem which is above, and like Sarah is free. Christians are the children of the promise, as was Isaac; but legalizers, like Ishmael, are the children of bondage. Legalizers who teach salvation by works are antagonists to Christians, and will be cast out by God. Paul declares of persons who are justified by faith, "So then, brethren, we are not children of the bondwoman, but of the free" (Galatians 4:31).

Hagar was a handmaiden to Sarah, and her purpose was to assist Sarah when she gave birth to the child of promise, Isaac. But when Abraham had a child through Hagar, she no longer served as Sarah's handmaiden but became critical of Sarah. The Law, symbolized by Hagar, was never intended to be a means of saving man. It was given by God to be the handmaiden to the gospel and to lead men to Christ by convicting them of sin and pointing up their need of a Saviour. The law was intended to bring men to Christ, who alone can save.

For man to turn to the works of the Law as the means of salvation is as wrong as Abraham's turning to Hagar as the means of producing the child of promise. When a man trusts his endeavor to keep the Law as the means of salvation rather than accepting the free gift of salvation through the cross of Christ, he goes the way of Hagar, the way of unbelief that declares, "I'll do it my way rather than God's way." To ignore God's way and to follow the course of unbelief and fleshly endeavor always result in personal disaster.

Sometime after World War II, a U. S. Air Force bomber was found in the middle of the Sahara Desert. On the fuselage were the words: *Lady Be Good.* One of the mysteries of the war was finally ended—*Lady Be Good*, the bomber that took off for a mission in North Africa and never was heard from again, had been found.

Investigators tried to determine why the plane was four hundred miles past its destination in the desert. The instruments were checked and were found to be still operating and accurate. The investigative team finally surmised that the plane had overshot its goal because it got into a high altitude air current that doubled its speed. The crew knew how long the flight ordinarily took, and when they reached their destination in half the time, they evidently assumed their instruments were in error and flew on. Eventually running out of fuel, they crash landed in the desert. A hundred miles from the plane, searchers found the remains of several of the crew who had perished trying to get help.

Lady Be Good, the plane whose crew apparently wouldn't believe its instruments, is an illustration of a world which is lost and perishing because it will not believe God's message of salvation through Jesus Christ. Unbelief is, more than anything else, a destructive force in the lives of those who cleave to it.

Detour of Unbelief

Chapter 6

Disclosed Road Map

*F*or thirteen years following the birth of Ishmael, God did not reveal Himself to Abraham. Because Abraham had failed to voluntarily wait upon God he was now forced to do so. He was ninety-nine years old before he heard God speak again (Genesis 16:16; 17:1).

How often has been proven true the saying, "Man's extremity is God's opportunity"! When Abraham reached his extremity and realized his helplessness, God moved in to manifest His grace and glory.

God always has good reason for the delays He allows to come into our lives. Scripture indicates that "the steps of a good man are ordered by the Lord" (Psalm 37:23). But included in God's guidance of His child are the "stops" as well. When things go well for us, it is easy to agree that our steps are ordered of God; however, when we come to "stops" in our lives we may feel that we are up against a blank wall with nowhere to turn. But that's a good position to be in.

Have you gotten yourself into a hopeless situation? If you're convinced of your weakness, then you're in a position to realize His all-sufficiency. Do you feel walled in on all four sides? Then look up and you'll discover that the roof is off and the light of God will shine upon you in a new way!

The long period of silence that exercised Abraham's heart was to him what the long winter is to the world of nature in preparing it for the outburst of spring.

After the thirteen-year stop in his life Abraham heard the voice of God again. And when God spoke He graciously manifested Himself. Rather than offering reproof, He offered divine love. God did not say, "Abraham, you're a failure!" He revealed Himself to Abraham under a new name, declaring, "I am the Almighty God [*El Shaddai*]" (Genesis 17:1). *El Shaddai* means "the all-powerful God, the all-sufficient God, the God who is more than enough."

Though time and circumstances seemed to indicate that God's covenant no longer could be fulfilled, God would prove Himself to be all-powerful; He would yet fulfill His pledge of a son for Abraham. The promise of worldwide blessing through Abraham's seed was irreproachable because it was the word of the omnipotent God!

Colonel Younghusband, an English officer, once made a hazardous journey into Tibet. He moved among the Tibetans with assurance in spite of great dangers. When someone asked him his secret he replied, "My secret is two-fold. I have been sent by an unimpeachable authority for a purpose which is sound; and if I get into a tight place, I have a government behind me which would use all its resources to see me through." Abraham's authority was the highest, and he had the government of the universe behind him to see him through.

What a grand summons Abraham received from God: "Walk before me, and be thou perfect" (Genesis 17:1). Three times in Scripture Abraham is called the friend of God (II Chronicles 20:7; Isaiah 41:8; James 2:23). Genesis 17; 18 reveal the elements of the friendship that Abraham shared with God. And the eternal God is willing to be to true-hearted saints in any age what He was to Abraham. Jesus Christ freely offers us the friendship of God (John 15:15).

We cannot comprehend why God deigns to seek our friendship. There is evidently in the heart of the Eternal a yearning for fellowship. F. B. Meyer, in *Abraham, Friend of God* (p. 84), attempts to explain why God should seek fellowship from fallen human creatures of earth:

Surely, if He had so desired it, He might have found—or if He could not have found, He might have created—a race more noble, more obedient, more sympathetic than ourselves. Or, at least, He might have secured one which should not cost Him so dearly, demanding of Him the anguish of Gethsemane, and the blood of the cross. So, perhaps, we are sometimes prone to think. And yet it could not be. That which is, and has been, must on the whole be the best that could be, since infinite love and wisdom have so ordered it. And perhaps none could be so perfectly the companions and fellows of the Son of God through all the ages as those who know the light, because they have dwelt in the darkness; who know the truth, because they have been ensnared in the meshes of the false; and who can appreciate love, because they have been in the far country, wasting their substance in riotous living, but have been redeemed by His blood.

The word "perfect" in Genesis 17:1 conveys the thought of moral completeness. It does not mean absolute sinlessness, which of course is impossible for any human. It denotes "wholeheartedness," the surrender of one's entire being to God. God is first in the thoughts, plans, pleasures, friendships, and actions of the man who walks with Him. God completely fills both his present and his future—his entire range of vision. His heart's desire is expressed by these words of the psalmist: "My soul, wait thou only upon God; for my expectation is from him. He only is my rock and my salvation: he is my defence; I shall not be moved" (Psalm 62:5,6).

Wholeheartedness is the quality of devotion that is ever dear to God. It is the primary characteristic noted by God in Noah and in Job (Genesis 6:9; Job 1:1,8). It is this quality that His eyes search for throughout the earth (II Chronicles 16:9).

"The world has yet to see what God can do with and for and through and in a man who is fully and wholly consecrated to Him." Dwight L. Moody heard Henry Varley make this statement at a meeting in Dublin in 1872.

The following Sunday, while he sat high up in Spurgeon's Tabernacle, those words of Varley ran over and over in Moody's mind. "The world has yet to see," Moody repeated to himself. "With and for and through and in a man! Varley meant *any* man! Varley didn't say he had to be educated, or brilliant, or anything else—just a man! Well, by the Holy Spirit in me, I'll *be* one of those men." And anyone familiar with the effects of the life and ministry of Moody will agree that he *was* one of those men.

Abraham was convinced that God must be in control, and he "fell on his face." What magnificent words we read next: "and God talked with Him" (Genesis 17:3). God desires to talk with men. He has provided fellowship with Himself through the Holy Spirit who imparts to us His Word. God's means for speaking to us today is the illumination of the Scriptures by the Spirit. The Christian can hear God speak to him daily when he reads the Bible.

When God spoke to Abraham, He unfolded a road map that outlined Abraham's destiny. Seven times God declared to Abraham, "I will." In like pattern He presented seven "I wills" in His call to Moses some 500 years later (Exodus 6:6-8). Seven is the perfect number in Scripture. God's call and promise to His servants is perfect!

Already God had presented His covenant to Abraham (Genesis 12:2,3; 13:14-17; 15:1-21). In this confirmation of the covenant He introduced two new features: He changed the names of Abraham and Sarah, and He established circumcision as the sign of the covenant.

The Abrahamic Covenant was given to Israel, the "New Covenant" to the church. Instituted by the same God as complementary phases of His redemptive program, the two covenants bear five comparable features.

First, both covenants involve a *world outreach.* In both Testaments of Scripture God has His arms reaching out to the whole world. To Abraham He promised, "Thou shalt be a father of many nations" (Genesis 17:4). And to His disciples Christ declared, "But ye shall receive power, after that the Holy Ghost is come upon you: and ye shall be witnesses unto me both in Jerusalem, and in all Judaea, and in Samaria, and unto the uttermost part of the earth" (Acts 1:8).

Speaking at a university, a philosopher recommended that in our minds we should get out of this world to see it. "For an understanding of the earth and its inhabitants, one should detach himself and get as far away as possible. There you get a larger pattern." There is no one better equipped to see the larger pattern that the Creator has for the whole world than the Bible believer. He is enabled through divine revelation to see the big view. He sees God and man, Heaven and Hell, time and eternity, sin and the redemptive program of God for a lost world.

Henry Martyn rightly declared: "The spirit of Christ is the spirit of missions; and the nearer we get to Him, the more intensely missionary we must become." And Robert E. Speer has resounded truthfully, "If you want to follow Jesus Christ, you must follow Him to the ends of the earth, for that is where He is going."

Every Christian can be in the mainstream

of God's worldwide program. This is possible through personal commitment to Christ; faithfulness in bearing the testimony of Christ in one's life; following God's leading in vocation and geographical location; stewardship of time, talents, and money in the ministry of the local church; discovery and deployment of spiritual gifts in the service of Christ; involvement in discipling other believers to become multiplying witnesses for Christ; study of church growth in the world; prayer for missions; and financial support of missionaries. The Great Commission is for every Christian! What place does world evangelization have in your life?

There is a progressive development in the promises God made to Abraham. In Haran God promised to make Abraham a nation. At Bethel the promise was to increase Abraham's seed as the dust of the earth. The first promise at Mamre was to multiply Abraham's seed as the stars. And now three times the patriarch is told that he will be the father of many nations. This innumerable multitude includes not only the Jewish nation but men of every nation who share Abraham's faith (Galatians 3:7-29).

Second, both covenants involve a *name change*. In the contract offered by God, Abraham and God became permanent partners. In memory of the moment, both Abraham and Sarah received new names (Genesis 17:5,15). To this point in their lives their names had been Abram and Sarai. Abram, which means "the father is exalted," is now changed to Abraham, "father of multitudes." Sarai is changed to Sarah, which means "princess." God's promise to Abraham and Sarah was that they would have a son and would become the father and mother of nations.

Under the new covenant the believer is born again into the family of God and has his name changed to "Christian." The believer meets God as a "sinner" and is made a "saint" through the blood of Christ.

Third, both the old and the new covenants carry the promise of a *land*. To Abraham was promised the land of Canaan: "I will give unto thee, and to thy seed after thee, the land wherein thou art a stranger, all the land of Canaan, for an everlasting possession" (Genesis 17:8). For the Christian also there is the promise of a land—an eternal dwelling place that Christ is preparing for those who know Him. Pity the soul who has seen only one life, and does not have in his heart the assurance of Heaven!

What a contrast there was between two men who approached death at the same time, one having lived his life for himself and the other having lived in the love of Christ. The first, upon hearing of the illness of his Christian friend, declared, "I will leave all my riches; but he will go to his riches."

Fourth, God has appointed a *seal* for both covenants. The insignia of the Abrahamic Covenant was the rite of circumcision. "Every man child among you shall be circumcised. And ye shall circumcise the flesh of your foreskin; and it shall be a token of the covenant betwixt me and you" (Genesis 17:10,11). Through circumcision God carved in the flesh of his people an unmistakable reminder of the holy relationship that they shared with Him. To the Jew circumcision meant separation from sin and the workers of sin, purity of life, and obedience to the will of God.

As the seal of the new covenant, the "holy Spirit of promise" is given to the Christian at the time of his conversion to Christ (Ephesians 1:13). The seal represents a finished transaction, divine ownership, and security.

Circumcision of the Abrahamic Covenant was a very intimate, personal experience. The seal of the Holy Spirit in the new covenant is likewise a very personal matter. Every child of the new covenant must personally experience the inner witness of the Holy Spirit (Romans 8:14-16). Do you personally have the inner witness of God's Spirit within your heart?

Fifth, both the old and the new covenants involve the promise of *a son.* Abraham was promised a son of Sarah: "I will bless her, and give thee a son also of her" (Genesis 17:16). Through that son was to come universal blessing. The ultimate manifestation of that blessing would be in Jesus Christ, the Son of Abraham and the Son of God. His eternal life is the gift of the new covenant.

When Abraham learned that the promised son would be born of Sarah, he "fell upon his face, and laughed, and said in his heart, Shall a child be born unto him that is an hundred years old? and shall Sarah, that is ninety years old, bear?" (verse 17). Abraham's laugh was not the sneer of unbelief but a spontaneous expression of delight at the promise of such an event.

Abraham still had hopes that Ishmael might be the one to fulfill the promises, as indicated by his statement to God: "O that Ishmael might live before thee!" (verse 18). Though this would be the natural solicitude of a parent, it was not according to God's plans. God's thoughts are not as man's thoughts. God promised that common blessings would be given to Ishmael (verse 20), but the blessings of the covenant were reserved for Isaac. "But my covenant will I establish with Isaac, which Sarah shall bear unto thee at this set time in the next year" (verse 21).

Abraham's immediate obedience and faith are seen in the ceremony of circumcision that he performed throughout his entire household following God's covenant message (verses 23-27). He believed God, and promptly acted on God's words.

Disclosed Road Map

Go, Abraham, Go

Chapter 7

Walking with God

*I*f two angels came to visit you, how would you treat them? What would be your feeling and response should Jesus Christ appear in visible form at your door?

The writer of Hebrews alludes to Abraham's experience in the command, "Let brotherly love continue. Be not forgetful to entertain strangers: for thereby some have entertained angels unawares" (Hebrews 13:1,2). We find God's presence in surprising people, in surprising places, and in surprising situations! Every person we meet is a potential conveyor of God's message to us.

Apparently, Abraham was unaware that the three strangers who appeared at his tent door in Mamre were visitors from Heaven (Genesis 18:1,2). But his affinity for Heaven was shown in his *commitment* to the supernatural visitors. The life of a man who walks with God is characterized by commitment.

When the heavenly messengers appeared, Abraham was sitting at a tent door in the fields, characteristic of his earthly sojourn with a heavenly vision (Hebrews 11:9,10). A contrast is apparent in the next chapter when the angels find Lot sitting "in the gate of Sodom" (Genesis 19:1).

An examination of the story before us reveals that the Lord Himself was one of the persons who appeared to Abraham (cf. Genesis 18:1,2,16,20; 19:1). This was a Christophany, a preincarnate appearance of Christ in visible form. Two thousand years later, when Christ declared to the Jews that He was from God, they asked, "Art thou greater than our father Abraham?" (John 8:53). Christ's response was, "Your father Abraham rejoiced to see my day: and he saw it, and was glad" (verse 56). Jesus was referring to His preincarnate manifestation of Himself to Abraham at Mamre. When the Jews questioned Christ's age, He declared, "Verily, verily, I say unto you, Before Abraham was, I am" (verse 58). By the words Christ used He indicated that Abraham was brought into existence but that He Himself had never come into being. He existed eternally before creation and will continue to exist eternally. Prior to His incarnation Christ sometimes appeared incognito in the lives of those He cherished as His friends.

How did Abraham respond to the heavenly guests? "He ran to meet them from the tent door, and bowed himself toward the ground" (Genesis 18:2). He pleaded with them to stay with him and called for water to wash their feet and for bread to refresh them. He prepared a feast for them. Abraham's first concern was not what he could get from the strangers but what he could give to them (verses 3-8).

Two millennia before Christ broke bread with the apostles, He feasted at Abraham's table. Abraham brought refreshment to the One he loved. Our lives always are a refreshment to our Lord when we love Him and serve Him.

Another characteristic of one who walks with God is *communion*. Because of his commitment Abraham was in a position to hear a special message from God—the promise of a son through Sarah (Genesis 18:9,10).

Overhearing the conversation from behind the tent door, Sarah could not muffle her laughter. She thought the promise was ridiculous (verses 10-12). She was an old woman now and it seemed biologically impossible for her to have a child. But when it became evident that the stranger was the Lord Himself, Sarah was afraid. The Lord rebuked her for her unbelief. "Is anything too hard for the Lord?" was the rhetorical question that the Lord posed to Abraham and Sarah (Genesis 18:14a). Sarah denied having laughed, but the Lord assured her that He knew she had laughed (verse 15).

Following the good news came bad news. God took Abraham into His confidence and revealed to him that He was going to destroy Sodom and Gomorrah. "Shall I hide from Abraham that thing which I do?" the Lord asked (verse 17). God chose to disclose His plan to Abraham because Abraham had an important part in that plan (verse 18), and because Abraham was committed to the ways of God—"For I know him, that he will command his children and his household after him, and they shall keep the way of the Lord" (verse 19).

To the man who communes with God, God imparts special insight concerning future events that the natural man does not understand. God shares His plan with the man who walks with Him. The committed disciple who is in communion with Christ understands Scriptural prophecy and shares a God-view of the world.

Had Abraham been living in Sodom he would not have been in a condition for receiving God's revelation. But because Abraham walked with God, God chose to disclose to him His divine plan. The way to understand the divine purpose for the world is not to be mixed up with the world but to be separated from it. The Christian is not simply a part of the world that bears witness to the truth of God, but he stands in the truth and bears witness to the world. One who walks with God is in a better position for understanding what is happening to the world than is any politician or king who doesn't know the Lord.

For Abraham communion with God resulted in *compassion* for condemned man. Here we see Abraham's outstanding intercession for Sodom. The man who is close to God will have a lost world close to his heart! True communion with God will not make us cloistered monks but will result in a concern for lost souls. True prayer will put a man to work quicker than any scheme religion can devise. Never should a church become so involved with itself that it turns in upon itself and forgets to reach out to the lost world. The church must gather to be edified, but it must scatter to evangelize.

When Abraham was left alone with the Lord, who had revealed that He would judge Sodom and Gomorrah (Genesis 18:20,21), Abraham "drew near" and interceded for Lot's city (verse 23). He pleaded with God not to destroy the righteous with the wicked. "Shall not the Judge of all the earth do right?" was his rational plea (verse 25). How swift God is to show mercy! When Abraham pleaded that the Lord spare the city if fifty righteous persons were found there, God agreed. And when Abraham lowered the number in successive pleas from fifty to forty-five, to forty, to thirty, to twenty, and finally to ten, God agreed each time (verses 24-33). The statement is true that "faith sees the invisible, believes the incredible, and receives the impossible."

We are not told why Abraham stopped at the number ten. It may be that God indicated ten was as far as He would go. There does come a limit to God's extension of grace. Or it may be that Abraham agreed if there were not at least ten righteous men in the city then he should not ask God to spare it for less. But not even ten righteous persons were found in the wicked twin cities, and God deemed it necessary to destroy the cities.

Under a picture of Peter Milne, the great missionary to the New Hebrides Islands, are these words: "When he came there was no light; when he died there was no darkness." Such is the story where Christ's light has been carried in the lives of men who walk with God.

Were it not for the purifying salt element

of Christians in Western civilization, God would find greater cause for destroying our society than He found in Sodom and Gomorrah. Little do ungodly men realize how much they owe to the presence of God's children in their midst. All the elements of ungodliness that were found in Sodom and Gomorrah are multiplied a thousandfold today. Even though Western civilization has a bright witness of the gospel, we continue to travel downward on a path of wickedness.

As purifying "salt" and as penetrating "light" (Matthew 5:13-16) Christians are set forth in the world to bear witness to the Saviour. When we walk with God we will have compassion for our world. What witness do you bear in the world? Has your "saltiness" had a purifying influence on others? What light have you shone into dark lives?

A factory that employed 500 men included a canteen and lounging room where men discussed topics of general interest following their lunch each day. One day the discussion centered on Christianity and hypocrisy, with some very harsh things being said about Christians. William James, a Christian in the company, could stand the criticism no longer. He spoke up: "Men, you have been saying some very hard things about Christians. Now I admit that there are hypocrites in the church, but I also want you to know that there are a lot of sincere Christians, and I, myself, very humbly claim to sincerely believe in Jesus Christ as my personal Lord and Saviour."

About to sit down, Bill heard a man say, "Just a minute, Bill, I would like you to answer some questions. I take it from what you have said that you believe the Bible to be the Word of God?"

"I certainly do," replied Bill.

"Then, do you believe that all men out of Christ are lost and on their way to outer darkness?"

"Yes, I do," he answered. And so the dialog proceeded:

"Do you think most of us men are out of Christ and therefore lost?"

"Yes, boys, I am very sorry indeed to say I do believe that."

"Do you believe in the power of prayer?"

"Yes, I have received many answers to my prayers in the past."

"Bill, how long have you worked here with us?"

"Four years."

"How often in that period have you spent a night in prayer for our lost souls?"

Bill's head didn't seem quite so high as he answered, "I am sorry, boys, but I cannot say I ever spent a night in prayer for you."

"Well, Bill, how often have you spent a half-night in prayer for us?"

"I am sorry, but I cannot say I ever spent half a night in prayer for you."

"Well, Bill, we'll take your word for it— quickly add together all the time you've spent in prayer for us during the last week; how much would it be, all told?"

"I am sorry, fellows, but I cannot say that I have spent any time in prayer for you this last week."

The questioner's last statement followed: "Well, Bill, that is just the kind of hypocrisy we've been talking about."

How our hearts should be rebuked when we claim to walk with Christ but do not have the compassion that Abraham bore in his intercessory prayer for Sodom and Gomorrah. Ours is the responsibility to pray for lost men and then to put feet to our prayers and seek to win them to the Lord Jesus Christ. Many bow their heads but few truly take the burden of lost souls upon their hearts.

William Cowper's words describing the power of prayer should still challenge us today:

Prayer makes the darkest cloud withdraw;
Prayer climbs the ladder Jacob saw,
Gives exercise to faith and love,
Brings every blessing from above.

Restraining prayer, we cease to fight;
Prayer makes the Christian's armor bright;
And Satan trembles when he sees
The weakest saint upon his knees.

Walking with God

Go, Abraham, Go

Chapter 8

End of the Dead-End Road

*W*hen Lot chose Sodom, he took a dead-end road. Sodom was a "sin city" that was destined for destruction. The message the heavenly ambassadors brought to Lot was, "We will destroy this place, because the cry of them is waxen great before the face of the Lord; and the Lord hath sent us to destroy it" (Genesis 19:13).

Sodom became synonymous with brazen sin (Isaiah 3:9; II Peter 2:6; Jude 7; Revelation 11:8). I once heard a news commentator in New Orleans declare, "Bourbon Street has a sin for every sinner." This was true of Sodom. Ezekiel lists the sins of Sodom as pride, prosperous complacency, and abomination (Ezekiel 16:49,50). The predominant sin presented in the story of the angels' visit there to rescue Lot is that of sexual perversion, particularly homosexuality. In fact, the word "sodomy" has come to represent the most debased forms of sexual perversion. Throughout the Scriptures homosexuality is condemned! It is never recognized as an acceptable form of "gay" living as some would have it today. And because of the wickedness of Sodom and Gomorrah, God brought destruction upon the twin cities.

The existence of the ancient cities of Sodom and Gomorrah is confirmed by an important archaeological discovery. In 1974, two Italian archaeologists discovered the 140-acre site of a kingdom called Ebla. Located in northwestern Syria, 150 miles west of Haran, Abraham's second home, Ebla dates from 3000 B.C. to 2000 B.C. To date archaeologists have dug on only one acre of the 140-acre site, and already have discovered Ebla's royal archives containing 18,000 cuneiform tablets covering a period from 2400 to 2250 B.C. The tablets reveal that Ebla was a city of 260,000, with a wide trading influence in the Middle East. To fully translate and index the tablets could take up to fifty years. But some Biblical information currently being translated from the tablets includes: 1) the mention of names of citizens later translated into David, Israel, Esau, Saul, and Abraham; 2) the frequent mention of Ebrium, or Eber, the same name as that of an ancestor of Abraham (Genesis 11:14-17); and 3) the documentation of trade by Ebla with a number of Old Testament cities and places, including Sodom and Gomorrah before their destruction.

Lot had become fixed in Sodom. The fact that he "sat in the gate of Sodom" indicates that he became a member of the municipal council, for the city gate in those days was the seat of civil government. The Nuzi documents indicate that all transactions involving transfer of property were witnessed and sealed at the town gate. For instance, Abraham's purchase of Machpelah was notarized at the city gate (Genesis 23:17,18).

God has two ways of bringing men to surrender to Himself. He may reveal to us the value of "things above" and draw us by the joys of Heaven. This He did with Abraham in Genesis 18. On the other hand He sometimes reveals to us the vanity of "things below" and drives us by the woes of earth. This He did with Lot in Genesis 19.

Peter reveals to us that Lot had been justified by God but was living in a miserable spiritual situation in Sodom. The filthy manner of life around him brought him constant distress of soul. "For that righteous man dwelling among them, in seeing and hearing, vexed his righteous soul from day to day with their unlawful deeds" (II Peter 2:8). Viewing Lot in Sodom, we discover three reasons for why a saint in Sodom is tormented.

A saint in Sodom is tormented because his *fellowship with the Lord is hindered.* The heavenly visitors found no comfort in Sodom as they had in Mamre. When Abraham invited the angels in, they happily consented. But when Lot invited them into his home for the night, they refused, until Lot finally pressured them into accepting his invitation (Genesis 19:2,3). It is most difficult for the backslider to enjoy fellowship with God, for God has no peaceful abiding place in the life of a worldly Christian.

Abraham was able to provide rest and

refreshment for the Lord and the angels at Mamre. But in Sodom, Lot brought danger to the angels. The men of Sodom surrounded the house and threatened to sexually assault the angels. "Where are the men which came in to thee this night? bring them out unto us, that we may know them" (verse 5). Today we need to remember what Lot had failed to realize—wherever we go, we take the Lord with us. If a place is not suitable for the Lord's presence, we should consider it unsuitable for ours and avoid it.

In Lot's experience we see another reason a saint is tormented in Sodom—*his testimony before man is lost.* Abraham had power with God in his intercession for his fellow man. But Lot had no power with his neighbors. When he pleaded with the wicked men of Sodom not to bother his visitors, they ridiculed him as a stranger who assumed more power than was rightly his. "They said, Stand back. And they said again, This one fellow came in to sojourn, and he will needs be a judge: now will we deal worse with thee, than with them. And they pressed sore upon the man, even Lot, and came near to break the door" (verse 9).

In setting forth the Christian as the salt of the earth, Christ declared, "but if the salt have lost his savour, wherewith shall it be salted? it is thenceforth good for nothing, but to be cast out, and to be trodden under foot of men" (Matthew 5:13). Lot had lost his saltiness in Sodom and now was trodden under foot. His lack of preserving influence is seen again when he warned his sons-in-law to flee from the city before it was destroyed. They ignored him "as one that mocked"—that is, one who had lost his senses (Genesis 19:14)—and perished in the holocaust.

The demoralizing influence of Sodom on Lot and his family is seen in a number of instances. His daughters had married men of the wicked city. The sons-in-law gave no serious attention to Lot's advice or warning. Lot's vicious offer of his daughters for immoral purposes is an indication of the influence that the wicked city had effected upon him. One cannot live in Sodom without feeling the effects of Sodom upon his life and his family. The pull of Sodom on Lot's wife was detrimental, resulting in her ignominious death. And the notorious sin of Sodom seriously affected Lot and his daughters, evidenced by their later acts of incest (verses 30-36).

Throughout our world we witness the tragic effects of the spirit of Sodom on the family and on modern morality. The "anything goes" attitude of society has led us into the misery that was brought to Sodom by its sin. A poll taken by the *National Enquirer* in November, 1976, revealed a widespread fear that the old foundations are crumbling and society desperately needs a return to respected, traditional standards. The *Enquirer* quotes Clare Boothe Luce, editor, playwright, former congresswoman, and former U.S. Ambassador to Italy, as follows:

> What we call the New Morality is actually the old immorality of decadent civilizations. And history shows that wherever the old immorality prevailed, the family was weakened and the society collapsed.

If the family is indeed the basic unit of civilized society, then one thing can be done: every mother and father must try to be a moral person in the traditional sense of the word.

Every parent must practice and teach morality within the family. If they do, America won't go down the drain. If they don't, America will have lost its heart and soul.

Again, Colonel Alex J. Stuart, president of the United States National Character Laboratory, is quoted as saying:

Sexual permissiveness destroys a person morally. I am very concerned that today's permissive, immoral outlook on life—especially among young adults—weakens and threatens the family structure which is essential to good character development.

We must return to the traditional American spirit of virtue and morality in order to produce future generations of decent people.

Rev. William McFadden, chairman of the Theology Department at Georgetown University, is quoted as follows:

Too often young people are looking for easy options. They try cohabitation rather than marriage without giving the proper concern to the future implications of such relationships. They should build a strong spiritual union.

A marriage based on spiritual love will be much stronger than one built on sexual attraction.

The basic building block of a strong society is the family unit. A return to the traditional standards of sexual morality would strengthen the family unit—and thus strengthen the country.

There are more divorces today than there have ever been before. There is more sexual permissiveness. And there is more blatant pornography in print and in other media. If God's destruction came upon Sodom for its flagrant iniquity, who are we to think that His judgment will not fall today?

You would think the historian Edward Gibbon was describing modern Western civilization when he gave the following reasons for the decline of the Roman Empire: 1) a rapid increase in divorce; 2) higher and higher taxes; 3) the intense craving for pleasure; 4) an emphasis upon armaments when the real enemy was the internal decadence of the people; and 5) the decay of religion, with faith becoming mere form. If Gibbon's analysis of Rome's fall is correct, we have cause to be seriously concerned about the fate of our society.

Arnold Toynbee once stated that there have been some twenty-four civilizations that developed, reached a peak, and then collapsed. Only three were conquered by outside invaders; the rest died from internal moral decay.

We are the recipients of much light from God through the spiritual heritage Western civilization has shared. To sin against such light makes us deserving of even greater judgment than that brought upon Sodom. It was to the enlightened city of Capernaum that Christ declared, "And thou, Capernaum, which are exalted unto heaven, shalt be brought down to hell: for if the mighty works, which have been done in thee, had been done in Sodom, it would have remained until this day. But I say unto you, That it shall be more tolerable for the land of Sodom in the day of judgment, than for thee" (Matthew 11:23,24).

A vulture was seen lighting upon a carcass on a slab of ice that floated downstream. The vulture kept eating the carcass until the ice came to a cataract. The vulture then lifted its wings to fly away, but because its claws had frozen to the ice it plummeted over the falls to its destruction. The sinner in Sodom indulges in sin with the thought that he can lift himself whenever he wishes; but he discovers too late that he is frozen to his little world and plunges to destruction.

There is a third reason a saint is tormented in Sodom—*his personal life is wasted.* Whereas Abraham received a promise of great blessing, Lot received only the warning of destruction (Genesis 19:13). So what if Lot had worked his way up to the city gate? All was lost!

More is said about Abraham in Hebrews 11 than about any other Bible character, but nothing is said about Lot. Nothing of his life was to be recorded in the "Hall of Faith." After his deliverance from Sodom, he faded into insignificance and is not mentioned again in the Old Testament. He was "saved; yet so as by fire" (I Corinthians 3:15). His personal life was wasted.

Lot, the man who followed the direction of his own selfish choosing, spent his last days cowering in a cave, stripped of everything, facing the results of his own shameful sin. Alexander MacLaren once advised, "If you're going to be your own Lord, then you must be your own slave!" Bondage to sinful flesh is the consequence of self-will.

When the body of the great missionary David Livingston was brought back to England, a man attending the funeral was in tears. His tearful confession was, "I knew David Livingston many years ago. Today I realize that I have lived my life for the wrong world." Surely this was the same confession Lot bore in the sad closing years of his life.

Archaeological investigation discloses the fact that during the middle of the twenty-first century before Christ, there was a catastrophe in the southern area of the Dead Sea which emptied the area of settled occupation for 600 years. The cause is said to have probably been an earthquake with an accompanying release and explosion of gaseous deposits.

The "slime pits" in the vale of Siddim (Genesis 14:10) actually were asphalt pits. In that area today is evidence of asphalt that was burned out. There is also evidence that sulphur hills and salt hills once surrounded the valley that is today nearly covered by the Dead Sea.

Running through Africa into the Dead Sea area is an earthquake fissure, indicating that a great earthquake shook the entire valley of Siddim, causing the ground to boil until the sulphur and salt hills melted into the asphalt as molten lava set fire to the asphalt and explosions took place. Molten brimstone was blown into the skies and rained down upon the citizens of Sodom and Gomorrah.

When Lot was hastened by the angels to leave Sodom, "he lingered." The angels "laid hold upon his hand" and "brought him forth, and set him without the city" (Genesis 19:15,16). The person saved by God's grace can be thankful that God has plucked him as a brand from the burning of eternal judgment.

Lot's wife delayed and was caught in the falling fire. Covered with salt and brimstone, she literally became a pillar of salt. She was so near deliverance, yet she delayed by looking back and "became a pillar of salt" (verse 26). Jesus warned us to remember Lot's wife and to beware lest the same fate overtake us because of lack of preparation for the coming judgment day (Luke 17:28-32).

1976 was reported to be the most disastrous year for earthquakes in the twentieth century. Could it be that God is warning us in this wicked age that the end is near? We have been given His word of warning in the Scriptures; but many disregard that word.

Some years ago on Long Island a man who purchased an expensive barometer eagerly unwrapped it when he got home, and in disgust put it down when he found the needle stuck at "Hurricane." In vain he shook it in an attempt to move the needle. He sat down and wrote an indignant letter to Abercrombie and Fitch, the makers of the barometer. When he returned from mailing the letter the "defective" barometer was gone, and so was his house—both having been destroyed in a hurricane!

God has given us His Word, not for observation but to be obeyed; not for consideration but that we might comply with it. We do well to believe and act when His "barometer" speaks.

Chapter 9

Relief from a Burdensome Load

*L*ong-standing sins must be uncovered and dealt with in the life God is to use! A sin may fester in the heart of a person for many years, breeding failure and sorrow because it is never judged. Abraham had harbored a sin for nearly thirty years. The sin then surfaced again and this time God delivered it the death blow. God always wants to work His maximum through us, but He can do so only when He reduces us to a minimum.

Abraham made another move, this time to Gerar. Why he moved we are uncertain. He may have been terrified by the destruction of Sodom. Or he may have been grieved at Lot's incest with Lot's daughters and the reproach that it brought to him. In any case, when he moved to Gerar, he revived an old sin that he first had committed during his sojourn in

Egypt because of the famine in Canaan.

You would think that by now Abraham would be determined never to lie again. But he did lie again. And the record of his lie is another indication of the divine inspiration of Scripture. If man had fabricated the story of Abraham's life, the natural inclination would have been to picture Abraham as one somewhat nearer perfection. But again, the Holy Spirit tells it like it was in Abraham's life.

In Genesis 20 we see Abraham's failure; but we also see God's faithfulness! Wouldn't you and I have given up in our spiritual venture were it not true that God is faithful in spite of our unfaithfulness? Abraham's repeated failures serve as a warning to us, but what God did for Abraham brings us great comfort.

For fear that Abimelech, king of Gerar, might kill him in order to take his beautiful wife, Abraham again resorted to carnal means of protecting himself rather than depending on God to do so. Abraham's later confession to Abimelech revealed that the lie he told had been connived in a compact that he made with Sarah nearly thirty years before he met Abimelech. "And it came to pass, when God caused me to wander from my father's house, that I said unto her, This is thy kindness which thou shalt shew unto me; at every place whither we shall come, say of me, He is my brother" (verse 13).

Abraham's lie was an indication of his faltering faith. Failing to trust God to take care of him, he resorted again to fleshly means of preserving himself. In his confession to Abimelech, Abraham revealed the fearful doubt that had prompted his lie: "Because I thought, Surely the fear of God is not in this place; and they will slay me for my wife's sake" (verse 11). Could not God care for Abraham in Gerar as He had done in Mamre? Indeed God is with us wherever we go. In the midst of a midweek trial we can trust God to be with us just as much as He is with us in a Sunday worship service.

Sometimes the sinner is a rebuke to the saint. When God caused Abimelech to realize his sin in pursuing Sarah, "Abimelech called Abraham, and said unto him, What hast thou done unto us? and what have I offended thee, that thou hast brought on me and on my kingdom a great sin? thou hast done deeds unto me that ought not to be done" (verse 9). God used the words of a sinner to rebuke Abraham for his sin!

I once heard the testimony of a man who became a Christian while he was serving in the United States Marine Corps. Some time following his conversion he prayed, "Lord, you've changed my life; you've made me a child of God. I do not yet know all that this entails. One of the things I'm wondering about right now is: am I supposed to cuss anymore? All the other marines do it, and it's been a natural part of my lifestyle. And I'm wondering whether I should continue cussing. I'm really sincere about this, and I pray that you will show me." Some time later this new Christian was talking with a fellow marine who was not a Christian, and he asked his fellow marine, "You know, I've become a Christian and I want the Lord to lead in my life. More than anything else I want to be a good witness to my fellow marines. Tell me, if you were a Christian, how would you be a witness to the other marines?" After reflecting for a few moments on the question, the fellow marine answered, "Well, first of all, I'd say, don't ever cuss!" What a clear answer to his prayer that was! And the answer came not from special revelation through a righteous channel, but through an unbeliever!

Sometimes the world has a better understanding of the standard for Christian living than does the Christian himself. A Christian's greatest rebuke may come not from another Christian but from the unsaved world. The reprimand that Abraham received for his sin came from the very place where Abraham feared God could not be present. Instead of being a witness to Abimelech, Abraham was rebuked by Abimelech.

Abraham's sin in Gerar was a carry-over of corruption. Although the Christian is called to "put off the old man" (Ephesians 4:22), he may continue to wear rags of corruption for a long time. One may not realize what is in his heart until circumstances arise to draw it out. A man's true character is manifested in time of trouble.

As long as Abraham lived under the compact that he had made with Sarah, he did not receive the blessing of a child through Sarah. Abraham had gone far with God and God had blessed him in spite of his iniquity. But now God put His finger on Abraham's sin. Finally the evil was dealt with and was removed. Abraham learned his lesson, and Isaac was born! Who knows what blessings of God may be withheld from our lives because of a long-standing sin in our hearts!

Although Abraham had lived with this sin in his heart for many years, he did not commit it often. When the occasion arose the sin popped up, but when there was no occasion, it lay dormant in Abraham's soul. We need to search our hearts for such sins, and render the death blow to them so that God can use us and bless us more fully.

God's faithfulness in Abraham's life is seen by the way he graciously overruled Abraham's act of unbelief. Although Abraham blundered, God prevented Abimelech from sinning against Sarah. Although Abraham entered Gerar with a lie; God entered Gerar with the truth. "God came to Abimelech in a dream by night, and said to him, Behold, thou art but a dead man, for the woman which thou hast taken; for she is a man's wife" (Genesis 20:3). Not only did God graciously overrule Abraham's lie, but He sovereignly controlled Abimelech's action. "For I also withhold thee from sinning against me: therefore suffered I thee not to touch her" (verse 6). How often the accounts in Scripture prove the proverb, "The king's heart is in the hand of the Lord, as the rivers of water: he turneth it whithersoever he will" (Proverbs 21:1).

God did not desert Abraham to his foes in Gerar. In Gerar, Abraham's sinful props were broken and he learned to lean solely upon God. When Martin Luther's friends wrote despairingly of the deliberations at the Diet of Worms, Luther replied from Coburg that he had been looking up at the stars of the night sky and had found no pillars to hold them up. And yet they did not fall, because God needs no props for His stars and planets. He hangs them on nothing. Likewise, in the working of God's providence, the unseen is prop enough.

In His faithfulness to Abraham God redemptively evaluated the situation in Gerar.

God presented Abraham to Abimelech as a prophet and made Abimelech a debtor to the prayers of Abraham. "Now therefore restore the man his wife; for he is a prophet, and he shall pray for thee, and thou shalt live: and if thou restore her not, know thou that thou shalt surely die, thou, and all that are thine" (Genesis 20:7). God did not view Abraham in his failure, but he saw Abraham as he was in God's redemptive plan—a prophet of God and a priest to Abimelech. How wonderful it is for the Christian today to know that he stands before the throne of grace, not in his own failure but in the success of Jesus Christ!

Not only is God's protection of Abraham seen in the restoration of Sarah to Abraham, but His providence is witnessed further in the material provisions that Abimelech made for Abraham (verses 14-16).

"So Abraham prayed unto God" (verse 17). No doubt Abraham's prayer included confession and cleansing. He realized the wrong that he had done and dealt with the matter before God. And his prayer was answered by the healing of the women of Abimelech's household that they might bear children (verses 17,18). As Abraham's prayer brought children to Abimelech, it also brought a child to Abraham (Genesis 21:1,2). After a long-standing sin was removed, a long-awaited blessing was received!

Abraham now was relieved from a burdensome load. Through God's gracious dealing with him in Gerar, Abraham now became a mature disciple. In all areas he now was surrendered to the will of God. In all responsibilities of life he now had a settled attitude of obedience.

Relief from a Burdensome Load

In the Waldensian valleys of Italy, the vines growing on huge wooden crosses are laden with grapes in September. The reason for this is the arms of the cross enable the branches to stretch out to receive every possible drop of rain and every ray of sun.

Fruit by means of a cross was the Saviour's design when He commanded His disciples to take up their cross and follow Him. God's formula for fruitfulness is the same in our lives as it was in Abraham's life. Upon the cross of commitment He reduces us to a minimum in order that He may produce in us His maximum. Francis Ridley Havergal summed it up well when she wrote:

Now, the pruning, sharp, unsparing;
Scattered blossoms, bleeding shoot!
Afterward, the plenteous bearing
Of the Master's pleasant fruit.

Chapter 10

Into the New Horizon

*T*hey waited twenty-five years from the time they left Haran before God's promise to them was fulfilled. Abraham was one hundred years old, and Sarah ninety, when God gave to them their son, Isaac. During the twenty-five years waiting period, God had made various promises to Abraham, but Sarah was not mentioned in relation to the promises for descendants until a year before Isaac was born. In God's own set time He faithfully fulfilled His promise. "And the Lord visited Sarah as he had said, and the Lord did unto Sarah as he had spoken. For Sarah conceived, and bare Abraham a son in his old age, at the set time of which God had spoken to him" (Genesis 21:1,2).

God is never too late. Though man may fret and worry and be in a hurry for plans to work out, God is in no hurry to work out His plans. God has an appointed time for accomplishing His will. While God waits for His appointed time, He tests the faith of man so it might be proved to be genuine. From the standpoint of human reasoning, a child for Sarah seemed like a foolish promise. But God is faithful. Nothing could hinder the outworking of His promise. "At the time appointed I will return unto thee, according to the time of life, and Sarah shall have a son" (Genesis 18:14). In God's time, *Isaac was born.*

Through Isaac the entire Hebrew nation was established in the earth. And God faithfully preserved Abraham's posterity for 2,000 years to serve as the channel for Jesus Christ the Messiah. The extensive character of God's miracle in the preservation of Abraham's seed is magnified by the story of Abraham Lincoln's short-lived posterity. Four children were born to the wife of Abraham Lincoln. One child died at age 4; another died at age 11; and a third died at age 18. Only one child, Robert Todd Lincoln, lived long enough to become married. He was the father of one son and two daughters. The son died before marriage, so the direct male line of Abraham Lincoln is today extinct. And the extinction took place in only three generations.

In contrast, God kept a fertile male for 2,000 years for the lineage of Christ. In addition, the posterity of Abraham is perpetuated as a vast nation in fulfillment of God's original promise to Abraham, "I will make of thee a great nation" (Genesis 12:2).

The birth of Isaac bears a number of similarities to the birth of Jesus Christ. Both were promised by God before their birth. For each there was a long period of waiting. The mother of each considered the promised birth to be an impossibility. Each of the two was named before his birth (Genesis 17:19; Matthew 1:21). For the birth of each there was a God-appointed time. Each of the births required a miracle—one mother was too old and the other was a virgin. Finally, each of the sons was his father's delight.

In Isaac we also view a picture of the sonship of the believer. Six phases of Christian experience may be illustrated in Isaac. First, the Christian experience begins with the impossible situation of *death*. "Old age" (Genesis 21:2) is the description of Abraham and Sarah at the time of Isaac's birth. The miracle involved in such a situation is described in Hebrews as follows: "Through faith also Sara herself received strength to conceive seed, and was delivered of a child when she was past age, because she judged him faithful who had promised. Therefore sprang there even of one, and him as good as dead, so many as the stars of the sky in multitude, and as the sand which is by the sea shore innumerable" (Hebrews 11:11,12).

When God brings salvation to a person He begins with the impossible situation of spiritual death. Before he is saved a person is "dead in trespasses and sins" (Ephesians 2:1). A skeptic once told an evangelist, "You talk about the burden of sin. I don't ever feel any burden of sin." The evangelist simply replied, "That's because you're spiritually dead and dead people don't feel burdens." Sad indeed is the fact that many people go through life spiritually dead without feeling the weight of iniquity that will carry them to eternal death. Only God can bring life to the spiritually dead.

The second phase of Christian experience illustrated in Isaac is that of *birth* (Genesis 21:3). Jesus said, "Except a man be born again, he cannot see the kingdom of God" (John 3:3). Out of the impossible situation of death, the Holy Spirit brings the believer to new life in Christ. Regeneration, not simply reformation, is what the human soul needs. A man once brought the hands of a clock to a clock repairman stating, "My clock is broken. The hands do not work. Please fix them." "Why didn't you bring the rest of the clock?" the repairman asked. The man replied, "The rest of the clock is working all right. The clock ticks well but the hands don't move." In a similar manner, men attempt to obtain salvation through outward reformation. One must do more than reform outwardly; he must be born again inwardly. Out of death there must come life; and only the Holy Spirit can bring that about.

Sanctification is the aspect of Christian experience illustrated in the circumcision of Isaac. "And Abraham circumcised his son Isaac being eight days old, as God had commanded him" (Genesis 21:4). Circumcision was commanded as the seal of the covenant with Abraham. The Holy Spirit is the "seal" of the believer, who is set apart unto God. Sanctification is the gradual inward transformation of the Holy Spirit resulting in purity, uprightness of character, and holy, spiritual thoughts expressing themselves in an outward life of godliness.

Isaac's *growth* illustrates a fourth aspect of

Christian experience. "And the child grew, and was weaned: and Abraham made a great feast the same day that Isaac was weaned" (verse 8). Spiritual growth is needed in the life of the believer. "But grow in grace, and in the knowledge of our Lord and Saviour Jesus Christ" (II Peter 3:18). Salvation is not merely a fire escape from Hell. God's plan for us is not that we remain babes in Christ; He wants us to develop into mature sons of God. The Christian's love is set upon Jesus Christ, and that love is ever growing.

A beautiful princess, according to an old story, was walking down a country lane when a handsome prince dressed in royal apparel met her, dropped on his knees, and proposed marriage. "If only I could have you for my bride," he said, "I would never want another. Will you give me your hand in marriage?"

Looking down at her new suitor, the princess replied, "Down the road about a mile my sister is following. She is far more beautiful than I. Go meet her and if after having seen her, you still desire me, I'll give you my answer."

The prince rose and ran down the road. About an hour later he returned with a look of great disappointment on his face. "Why did you tell me that your sister was more beautiful than you?" he asked. "She's not to be compared with you in beauty."

The princess replied, "I know that, but didn't you say that if only you could have me you would never want another? If that is true, why did you even bother to go look at my sister?"

Having expressed his love for the Son of God, the believer must not follow after some other love and become unfaithful and inconsistent in his devotion to his Saviour. The affirmation of the growing Christian is:

I have heard the voice of Jesus,
Tell me naught of else beside.
I have seen the face of Jesus,
And my soul is satisfied.

Conflict is the fifth aspect of Christian living illustrated in the life of Isaac. "And Sarah saw the son of Hagar the Egyptian, which she had born unto Abraham, mocking" (Genesis 21:9). Ishmael represented the "flesh," and Isaac represented the "spirit." The conflict between Ishmael and Isaac demanded that they be separated. Their conflict is a picture of the conflict between the old and new natures in the life of the believer. Some believers think there can be harmony between the old and new natures. Abraham thought at first that his two sons could live together in harmony. But the time finally came when Abraham realized that harmony was impossible and that a choice had to be made. And so it is with the Christian life. A choice must be make between sin and righteous living.

The sixth aspect of Christian living illustrated here is *victory*. Abraham finally did as God commanded and sent Ishmael away (verse 14). For present-day believers the struggle with the flesh is intense, but to cling to the flesh results only in bondage. The Christian must exercise discipline so he is not entangled again with the yoke of bondage. He is to separate himself from the things of the world and to please Christ in all that he does.

"Knowing this, that our old man is crucified with him, that the body of sin might be destroyed, that henceforth we should not serve sin" (Romans 6:6).

A deacon asked a young girl who was being examined for membership in a local church, "Has Christ made a difference in your life?" She replied that He certainly had. Attempting to draw her out more, he asked, "Well, then, do you sin anymore?" The girl admitted that she did. The next question was, "Well, if you continue to sin since you became a Christian, how has Christ made a difference in your life?" After reflecting for a moment, the girl replied, "Sir, I think it is this: before I was a Christian I ran after sin. Now I run from it, though sometimes I am still overtaken."

With his son Isaac, the gift of God's promise, Abraham entered into the new horizon in his walk with God. Because he was true to God in his walk of faith, Abraham received Abimelech's clear recognition of the fact that God was with Abraham. Abraham and Abimelech made a peace covenant at the well of Beersheba (Genesis 21:22-32). "And Abraham planted a grove in Beer-sheba, and called there on the name of the Lord, the everlasting God" (verse 33).

Chapter 11

Mountain of Testing

*T*he next sound of God's voice in Abraham's life brought him to the high watermark of his career. At Gerar Abraham's long-standing sin had been settled and the long-awaited blessing had been realized. But "after these things" followed the severest test of Abraham's life (Genesis 22:1). Times of special blessing frequently are followed by severe tests. Trial is necessary for the believer because it proves whether or not his spiritual experiences truly have become a part of his life and character. God sends us no trial without first preparing us. His testing is His vote of confidence in the believer.

"God did tempt Abraham" (verse 1). God put Abraham to the supreme test to prove whom he loved most. The devil tests men to bring out the evil that is in their hearts, but God tests His saints in order that He may bring forth all the good. Trials often call to the front latent qualities produced by grace but not yet brought into exercise in the Christian's life. Trials bring the believer to a plateau of life from which he is able to take a wider view and climb to further heights of godly experience.

If God had asked Abraham to sacrifice Eliezer, his faithful and beloved slave, the trial would have been difficult enough. A demand for Ishmael, the son of Hagar, would have been even more unbearable. But God's requirement was the supreme demand: "Take now thy son, thine only son Isaac, whom thou lovest, and get thee into the land of Moriah; and offer him there for a burnt-offering upon one of the mountains which I will tell thee of" (verse 2). We can hardly imagine the grief Abraham must have felt as he puzzled, "Why would God demand the sacrifice of my long-expected son?"

Any parent would agree there is a sacrifice greater than laying down one's life—it is the surrendering of someone who means more than life itself. To be asked to give up a son upon whom the sun rises and sets is indeed a traumatic experience. But God sometimes asks of us what He asked of Abraham. The specifics may vary, but His requirement is the same—the surrender of whatever means the most to us.

God's request for the sacrifice of Isaac raised a serious question concerning His former promise: "In Isaac shall thy seed be called" (Genesis 21:12). How could God's promise be fulfilled if Isaac were dead? The answer lies in Abraham's belief in the resurrection. Abraham believed that God would bring Isaac back to life after he was offered. Hebrews 11:17-19 reveals Abraham's conviction: "By faith Abraham, when he was tried, offered up Isaac: and he that had received the promises offered up his only begotten son. Of whom it was said, that in Isaac shall thy seed be called: Accounting that God was able to raise him up, even from the dead; from whence also he received him in a figure." Abraham's statement at the foot of Mt. Moriah was an indication of his belief in the resurrection: "I and the lad will go yonder and worship, and come again to you" (Genesis 22:5). Abraham viewed his activity as "worship," and he expressed faith that he would not ultimately lose Isaac.

Abraham's trip to the sacrificial altar on Moriah is an example of faith in its highest sense. Abraham was called to prove that he loved God more than he loved the things of this life, and even more than he loved any other person. Though human sacrifices were a common practice of heathen people in Abraham's time, such sacrifices were not intended by God. In fact, the Scriptures record no other incident where God tested a believer by calling him to make a human sacrifice. But God chose this test for Abraham to prove whom he loved most. God already knew what Abraham would do, and He knew that He Himself would provide a ram to take Isaac's place. And no one could receive a truer approval of faith than the declaration Abraham heard from God: "Now I know that thou fearest God" (verse 12).

Abraham had proved that he was ready to have his life cleared of all but God and His will. This was the final triumph of grace in

Abraham's pilgrimage. After receiving the promised son, Isaac, Abraham had been tempted to give more of his attention to the gift than to the Giver. But the supreme test into which God had brought Abraham was to teach Abraham to keep his attention on the One who performed the miracle, rather than on the miracle itself.

The following quaint sign was seen in the window of a dry cleaning and dyeing business: "We dye to live, we live to dye; the more we dye, the more we live; and the more we live, the more we dye." The New Testament teaches that, for the child of God, the more he dies, the more he lives. Jesus gave this illustration of that truth: "Except a corn of wheat fall into the ground and die, it abideth alone: but if it die, it bringeth forth much fruit" (John 12:24).

When asked about the secret of his marvelous fruitfulness as a Christain, George Muller replied, "There came a day when George Muller died, utterly dead! No longer did his own desires, preferences, and tastes come first. He knew that from then on Christ must be all in all!" Only when the believer thus renounces his self-centered inclinations can he experience the fruitfulness of Christ in his life. Abraham died to himself when he responded to God's call to sacrifice Isaac.

God's command to Abraham to offer Isaac is the only Old Testament story which distinctly intimated that God's requirement for our salvation involves a human sacrifice. Notice the parallels between Abraham's offering of Isaac and the heavenly Father's offering of His son, Jesus Christ, as our Saviour.

Isaac was Abraham's *only son:* "Take now thy son, thine only son Isaac, whom thou lovest" (Genesis 22:2). Can you imagine how every phrase of God's command stabbed Abraham's heart as he heard it? Two thousand years later God Himself experienced the agony of such a sacrifice. "For God so loved the world, that he gave his only begotten Son, that whosoever believeth in him should not perish, but have everlasting life" (John 3:16).

Abraham was prompt in his response to God's command. He "rose up early in the morning" (Genesis 22:3). He did not stall for time by consulting other people about the matter, nor did he try to reason things out in his own mind. He quickly obeyed God's command, "Get thee into the land of Moriah; and offer him there for a burnt-offering upon one of the mountains which I will tell thee of" (verse 2).

Notice there was a designated *hill* for the sacrifice. Appropriately, Mt. Moriah was the place where the temple of Solomon was later erected, and where thousands of animal sacrifices were offered as types of Christ, "the Lamb of God, which taketh away the sin of the world" (John 1:29). The place designated for the crucifixion of Christ was also a mountain—Mt. Calvary— outside the ancient wall of Jerusalem. "And when they were come to the place, which is called Calvary, there they crucified him" (Luke 23:33).

The sacrifice of Isaac required a *mutual agreement* between Abraham and his son. Abraham told the two young men whom he left at the foot of Moriah, "I and the lad will go yonder" (Genesis 22:5). As Isaac and his father were leaving the young men, Isaac asked, "Behold the fire and the wood: but where is the lamb for a burnt-offering?" (verse 7). He probably knew that he was to be the sacrifice, but he willingly went along with his father (verse 8).

The provision of salvation through Christ's death was made by a divine transaction between the Father and the Son. The submission of Jesus Christ to the will of the Father in coming to earth to die for men's sins is depicted by the writer of Hebrews: "Wherefore when he cometh into the world, he saith, Sacrifice and offering thou wouldest not, but a body hast thou prepared me. . . . Lo, I come (in the volume of the book it is written of me,) to do thy will, O God" (Hebrews 10:5,7).

Judgment by the father is depicted in Abraham's act: "And Abraham built an altar there, and laid the wood in order, and bound Isaac his son, and laid him on the altar upon the wood. And Abraham stretched forth his son, and took the knife to slay his son" (Genesis 22:9,10). But Abraham's hand was stayed. Having proved Abraham's faith, God provided a substitute for Isaac. The sacrifice was completed, but a ram was killed in the place of Isaac (verse 13).

God spared Abraham heart pangs that He could not spare Himself when the time came for His Son's crucifixion. Because it was necessary that Christ die for our sins, and because no other means of salvation was possible, Christ was "smitten of God, and afflicted. . . . and the Lord hath laid on him the iniquity of us all" (Isaiah 53:4,6).

God did not call off the sacrifice, but He provided a *substitute* for Isaac. While

Abraham and Isaac were walking up one side of the mountain, up the other side God was bringing a ram that would be in the thicket ready to take Isaac's place. How exhilarated Isaac must have felt when he learned that God had provided a ram to be offered in his place. But infinitely greater is the appreciation the Christian should have for the divine substitute "who his own self bear our sins in his own body on the tree, that we, being dead to sins, should live unto righteousness: by whose stripes ye were healed" (I Peter 2:24).

Abraham is one of the most positive Biblical examples of a good father. God's recognition that Abraham loved Isaac is the first actual mention of "love" in the Bible. Abraham's close companionship with Isaac indicates that no "generation gap" existed between the two even though Abraham was 100 years older than his son. We see that Abraham desired God's best for Isaac—he dismissed Ishmael when God warned him that Ishmael would thwart the divine purpose for Isaac. Also, Abraham obeyed God in his offering of Isaac at Moriah; but he believed God would resurrect Isaac so that God's promise might be fulfilled in Isaac. The trip Abraham and Isaac took together to Moriah further indicates a close relationship between Abraham and his son. We also see that Isaac was a disciplined, obedient lad, for he was submissive to the sacrifice plan when Abraham revealed it to him at Moriah. And in his concern for Isaac's comfort and care after Sarah's death, Abraham made provision for Isaac's marriage. In many respects Abraham was a wonderful example of what every father should strive to be.

Chapter 12

Beyond the Horizon

At the age of 127, thirty-seven years after the birth of Isaac, Abraham's wife Sarah died (Genesis 23:1,2). Yet even in this trying time, Abraham's neighbors knew where he stood with God. Although Abraham mourned and wept at Sarah's death, he looked beyond the grave to the resurrection. His tears sparkled with genuine *hope.* The sorrow of the believer is unlike that of "others which have no hope" (I Thessalonians 4:13). Standing in the shadow of death, Abraham declared to his neighbors, "I am a stranger and a sojourner with you" (Genesis 23:4). This testimony clearly indicated that Abraham looked forward to a better country prepared by God (Hebrews 11:14-16). He was a sojourner with a sure destiny.

Michael Farraday was once asked, "What

121

are your speculations about death?" His response was: "Speculations? I have no speculations. I have certainties!" He then quoted the basis of his hope, "I know whom I have believed, and am persuaded that he is able to keep that which I have committed unto him against that day" (II Timothy 1:12). And such a hope caused Abraham to prepare for Sarah's body a waiting place for the resurrection.

Abraham maintained an attitude of *humility* before his neighbors. He referred to himself as a sojourner, even though he was a man of much wealth, indicating that he had not allowed himself to become attached to worldly possessions. He confessed that he was a stranger even when his neighbors declared, "Thou art a mighty prince among us" (Genesis 23:6). Although Abraham stood in the threefold commanding position of a great man, an aged patriarch, and a mourner, he humbly "bowed himself to the people of the land" (verses 7,12). Probably Abraham had done many helpful things for the people, and was honored by them, yet he would not accept land without paying for it.

A farmer once commented to his son as they walked through the wheat fields: "Notice that the stalks of wheat that stand straight and tall are light-headed. The grain is very little inside the husks on these stalks. But notice the stalks that are bending over." Peeling the top of one of these stalks, the farmer showed his son a large golden grain of wheat. "Son, that's a lesson on life. Those who stand straight and proud and do not humble themselves before God are light-headed people, but those who have true inward character will humble themselves be-

122

fore God and others." In the painful day of his wife's death, Abraham manifested hope and humility.

A third character trait Abraham manifested at the time of Sarah's death was *honesty.* Although the sons of Heth offered to give him any land he wanted for a burying place for Sarah, Abraham refused to be indebted to his ungodly neighbors. He let it be known that he was a separated man and intended to stay in his separated position. Carefully weighing his payment for the land before witnesses, Abraham paid for ground containing the cave of Machpelah, where he buried Sarah (verses 9,16,19). Because Abraham's worship in Moriah had been real, his walk in Hebron was honest. And likewise, the Christian today is to "provide things honest in the sight of all men" (Romans 12:17).

The cave purchased by Abraham for Sarah's burial later was to become his burying place also (Genesis 25:7-10). His purchase indicated that he planned to stay in the land of Canaan rather than return to Mesopotamia, and it confirmed his declaration of faith in God.

Abraham also declared his faith when he sent for a bride for Isaac. Oriental custom gave the father the responsibility to find a suitable bride for his son and to make necessary arrangements with the woman's parents for the marriage. The arrangements were usually made through a representative who interceded on behalf of the son. Abraham was greatly concerned that a wife for Isaac not be taken from the unbelieving people of Canaan, so he sent Eliezer his servant to Mesopotamia to find a wife for his son (Genesis 24:1-9).

As marriage is a type of the relationship of
Christ and the church (Ephesians 5:23-33),
Eliezer's search for a bride for Isaac serves as a
splendid illustration of the ministry of the
Holy Spirit in bringing the bride of Christ to a
faith relationship with the Saviour. Jour-
neying to Nahor, Eliezer prayed for God to
show him who the bride should be, and he
placed himself in the proper position for
discovering the woman whom God would
choose for Isaac. Because he fulfilled his
responsibility, Eliezer was later able to declare, "I being in the way, the Lord led me"
(Genesis 24:27). When Rebecca came to the
well, she consented to provide water for
Eliezer and offered to fetch water for the
camels as well, unconscious that she was fulfilling the conditions that indicated she was
the Lord's choice for Isaac (verses 14-26).
Eliezer generously responded to Rebecca's
kindness and made her a gift of "a golden
earring . . . and two bracelets for her hands"
(verse 22). These gifts that any young woman
would treasure were not only an expression of
appreciation, but they also indicated the
stature and wealth of Abraham and Isaac.

Like Eliezer, the Holy Spirit does not speak
of Himself but of another whom He represents. The Holy Spirit sets before us the
blessings of union with Christ. Speaking of
the Holy Spirit's ministry Christ declared,
"He shall glorify me: for he shall receive of
mine, and shall shew it unto you" (John
16:14).

Eliezer was faithful in his mission. He
declared that he would not eat until he had
spoken of his errand (Genesis 24:33). What if
Rebecca had rejected Eliezer's offer? Abra-

ham had declared that Eliezer's job would be completed even if the woman would not be willing to follow him (verse 8). The servant's job would be completed even if his offer were rejected. The same is true in the Holy Spirit's provision of salvation to man. God has warned, "My spirit shall not always strive with man" (Genesis 6:3). Someday the Holy Spirit's work will be done, regardless of man's acceptance of His message.

How beautiful is the story of Rebecca's acceptance of the servant's invitation! She ran ahead of Eliezer to inform her household of his visit. Rebecca's family warmly welcomed Eliezer, inviting him to "come in, thou blessed of the Lord" (Genesis 24:31). Evidently Abraham's kinsmen also had come into the knowledge of the one true God. Abraham had been a fruitful witness for the Lord before he left home.

After Eliezer reviewed all the facts of the reason for his journey, the events at the well, and the guidance of God (verses 34-49), Rebecca's family was convinced that "the thing proceedeth from the Lord" (verse 50). Though they agreed that Rebecca could become the wife of Isaac, they sought some way to delay Rebecca's departure. But the question was left to Rebecca, "Wilt thou go with this man? And she said, I will go" (verse 58).

The person to whom the Holy Spirit speaks concerning the things of Christ must respond "I will." Though we, like Rebecca, have never personally seen our lover, we are wooed by the Holy Spirit and respond to His call to go to Christ, "whom having not seen, ye love; in whom, though now ye see him not, yet believing, ye rejoice with joy unspeakable and full of glory: Receiving the end of your faith, even the salvation of your souls" (I Peter 1:8,9). Today the church, under the guidance of the Holy Spirit, goes forward to meet the heavenly Bridegroom. How rapturous will be her experience when she sees her Bridegroom coming to meet her and is joined to Him eternally in inseparable love! The joy of the union of Rebecca and Isaac, though captivating in its Scriptural narration, cannot compare to the joy of the union of the church with Christ (Genesis 24:61-67; Revelation 19:7-9).

Abraham himself experienced the joy of remarriage. During his marriage of some thirty years to Keturah he was blessed with six sons (Genesis 25:1-11). This was in part a fulfillment of God's promise that he would be the father of a multitude (Genesis 13:16; 17:6,7).

At the end of Abraham's long life of glorifying God, he "gave up the ghost, and died in a good old age, an old man, and full of years; and was gathered to his people. And his sons Isaac and Ishmael buried him in the cave Machpelah" (Genesis 25:8,9). The blessings promised to Abraham continued in Isaac: "And it came to pass after the death of Abraham, that God blessed his son Isaac" (verse 11). Not only did Abraham begin well, he also ended well.

Throughout his lifetime Abraham was a "man on the go." Obedient to the call of God, he pursued God's purpose in his life. Stumbling in his humanity, he grasped for God's power in his life. His faith in God is the key to his success. Through Abraham's faith came Israel, the Messiah, and the church! "So then they which be of faith are blessed with faithful Abraham . . . and if ye be Christ's, then are ye Abraham's seed, and heirs according to the promise" (Galatians 3:9,29). Abraham is the father of the faithful ones. The Christian today joins an innumerable host who sing, in the words of Thomas Olivers (c. 1770):

The God of Abram praise,
Who reigns enthroned above,
Ancient of everlasting days,
And God of love:

Jehovah! Great I AM!
By earth and heav'n confessed;
I bow and bless the Sacred Name,
For ever blest.